BALZAC

A CRITICAL STUDY

de Balzac

BALZAC
A CRITICAL STUDY

By

HIPPOLYTE ADOLPHE TAINE

Translated, with an Appreciation of Taine, by
LORENZO O'ROURKE

FUNK & WAGNALLS COMPANY

NEW YORK AND LONDON

1906

CONTENTS

CHAPTER   PAGE

     An Appreciation of Taine 9

     BALZAC: A CRITICAL STUDY 83

I.   His Life and Character 85

II.   The Genius of Balzac 109

III.   Balzac's Style 135

IV.   The World of Balzac 163

V.   The Great Characters 189

VI.   Balzac's Philosophy 217

AN
APPRECIATION OF TAINE

AN APPRECIATION OF TAINE

A BIOGRAPHICAL study of the greatest of novelists by the most eminent of modern critics can hardly fail of interest in a country in which the names of Taine and Balzac have been adopted, as it were, into the national literature. The author of "The Human Comedy" has become a household word among the English speaking peoples, while the name of Taine, made hardly less popular by reason of the masterly "History of English Literature," is held in equal honor. Of the two, Balzac is by far the more intimately known, the events of his life having been described with as much detail as he himself lavished upon the characters of his mimic world.

With Taine the case is entirely different. Of all the famous men of his time, he is the least intimately known. He seems to

9

have cared absolutely nothing for fame,
and had supreme contempt for its coun-
terfeit, notoriety. Abnormally modest and
retiring in disposition, he shrank from
publicity as from the breath of contagion,
and succeeded in keeping his private life
completely veiled, even after he had attained world fame. His ideal, no doubt,
would have been a biography in the style
of Shakespeare, in which all that was
known of his life might be written in a
page.

When on March 5, 1893, the news of
Taine's death was telegraphed throughout the world, the last of a great group
of French writers had passed away, and
the history of French literature in the
Nineteenth Century might be written.
Renan had died six months earlier, so
that France was deprived of her two
greatest men almost at a stroke. The
news of Taine's death caused intense interest in this country, but, in spite of his
great celebrity, the obituary accounts were

singularly scant of facts. It then dawned upon Taine's admirers that his reputation was strangely disproportionate to the known facts of his life. Since then curiosity has been busy with research, and to-day it is possible, by reason of his correspondence, to gain a relatively satisfactory knowledge of the facts in his career.

I

Taine is the type and embodiment of that form of materialist determinism which the definitive overthrow of the old ideas by historical criticism, comparative philology, and the modern conception of evolution, established to so large an extent in the learned world. His method exhibits a temperament in which science, wholly dominant, excludes the spiritual from the conception of life. In Taine the modern materialist type achieves completeness, while the spiritual has reached its nadir. He is the creative literary artist of the laboratory, the alchemist of modern thought, whose ingenious and persistent search for truth rivalled the historic quest of the alchemists for gold. His prose has the glittering beauty of the flame blooms of the crucible. He is the anatomist of literature under whose jeweled scalpel

modern thought is revealed in forms of
striking originality.

Taine's achievement in history, philosophy and criticism may be said to match
Zola's in the field of fiction, for the methods of the realist of romance and the realist of science were singularly alike. The
characteristic traits, in fact, are identical:
unrivalled power of analysis, a genius for
detail, and a philosophy of stark materialism unrelieved by a ray of the ideal. The
descriptive prose of Taine is suggestive
of the realistic and graphic paintings of
Meissonier, in which a blade of grass is as
perfectly depicted as the silhouette of Napoleon. To this species of mind there is
neither great nor small; an atom is equal
to a world: hence infinite care for detail
arriving almost at infallibility within its
peculiar sphere. Taine approaches the
problems of philosophy, equipped with
microscope and alembic. The seer's vision is replaced by the methods and instruments of the anatomist and chemist. In

the hands of Taine science becomes magic.

Master of an original and striking style, he advanced as with a stride to the forefront of French letters. Out of the opulent and multi-colored French language he fashioned an instrument of wondrous potency. Clear, exact, enriched with an abundance of illustration that has never been surpassed, his writings make an effective appeal to the modern mind. He is a multi-millionaire of ideas, the spoil of many literatures and sciences,—of philosophy, art, history, philology, biology. Probably with the exception of Balzac and Victor Hugo, no other writer succeeded in gaining so perfect a mastery over the French language, with its delicacy, its nuances, its infinite variety. Such a writer loses in translation, however faithful. It is impossible to transplant with entire success ideas sprung from so rich a soil.

This luminous intellect, capable of reflecting truth in its myriad phases, and ever striving to pierce to the heart of its mystery, had, it must be acknowledged, a serious defect. With all its brilliance and wealth of metaphor, his prose sometimes leaves the reader cold. Saintsbury has applied a peculiar epithet to his style. He calls it "hard and brassy." One sometimes feels that the milk of human kindness has been dried up by the blaze of intellect, that the poet has been annihilated by the savant. Even his beautiful passages have at times the taint of the laboratory. The descriptions of natural beauty are often catalogs rather than canvases, heaped up with details painfully elaborated,—mosaics, which appeal to the mind, never to the heart. At times his pages remind us vividly of what we see in the kaleidoscope —of those pictures hard, glittering, and highly interesting, composed of the fortuitous contributions of a thousand colors and figures, ever changing, always revealing finished forms,—exact, sudden, brilliant, without inspiration, but compelling attention and admiration. This glorified kaleidoscope of thought is revealed in contrasts so dazzling, and is at times so elaborate, that it imposes upon us for beauty. Taine is a kind of surgical Victor Hugo armed with microscope, alembic and scalpel, but lacking the poet's Olympian imagination. At times his sentences are so striking, so poignant, that they suggest the possibility of his having studied with profit the greatest of modern Frenchmen. In Taine's most popular writing, as in Hugo's, the interest never flags. This is incomparable merit. The opulence of his illustrations and his display of learning tempt one to compare him with Rabelais. Certainly no modern is to be named with him in this respect, and his primacy in technical and general erudition has been freely acknowledged by his enemies.

His appetite for detail was insatiable. No modern writer ever massed such quantities around a fact. This is what invests his writings with so interesting a quality, notwithstanding his hard, uncompro-

mising method and his lack of human
sympathy. His prose has the same at-
traction as an intricate original piece of
machinery. It extorts admiration by reason of the fine adjustment of its parts, and
by its highly wrought and rigorous mechanism. But the human sympathies are
seldom stirred. Taine, indeed, is not con-
cerned about them. At times the hard,
flint-like brilliance of his thought becomes
almost painful; it sears like the glare of
dry sun-rays from polished rocks. We
can not resist the suspicion that this arid
quality has had a large share in influenc-
ing his judgments of historical person-
ages, and of the human drama which has
formed the subject of his constant meditations.

Hippolyte Adolphe Taine was born on
April 21, 1828, at Vouziers, Ardennes,
France. He was descended from a rug-
ged burgher stock, which for generations
had been distinguished by traits of hon-

esty, intelligence, and morality. Pierre
Taine, his great-grandfather, was a man
of superior intelligence, whose acquire-
ments and tastes had gained for him in
his little provincial world the nickname
of *the philosopher*. What is still more
significant is the fact that Hippolyte
Taine's maternal grandfather, M. Bezanson, was distinguished for scientific tastes,
and was deeply interested in the then bud-
ding theories which were to attain their
full flower in the Nineteenth Century, and
in whose fruitful fields his grandson was
to play so important a part. This immedi-
ate ancestor of Taine was in advance of
his time, and it is interesting to observe
how his tastes and achievements were a
prelude to those of his distinguished descendant. If he had lived a century later
it is hardly doubtful that he would have
achieved a high reputation as a scientist.
He was a profound student, not only of
philosophy and the mathematical sciences,
but of magnetism, which had appeared as

a startling revelation on the horizon of
knowledge. This fascinating science, with
its nimbus of mystery and quasi-magic,
must have had a deep charm for the grandfather of Taine. That the memory of the
scholar-grandfather was a cherished one,
is proved by the fact that Taine religiously
preserved treatises of philosophy and
mathematics written by the old man in his
ripe age.

Jean Baptiste Antoine Taine, father of
Hippolyte Taine, was a man of culture
and refinement, a country lawyer, who in
the intervals of professional labor, pre-
sumably not too exacting, devoted himself to the cultivation of literature and
the study of nature. He had a reputation
as a poet and wit, and his lyrical compo-
sitions and ballads were remembered and
repeated by the whole countryside years
after his death. He had a passionate love
for his son, and lavished upon him an
affection and care that suggest a presci-
ence of the destiny in store for the intelli-

gent youth. He taught the boy the rudi-
ments of Latin and the sciences. It was,
therefore, under the tutelage of a tender
father, among the charming scenes of
nature and in the atmosphere of innocence
that the young Taine laid the foundation
of the immense erudition afterward acquired. The slight sketch that we have
of this admirable father suggests a de-
lightful and charming personality. Without question the influence thus exerted on
the son was deep and permanent.

Taine's mother was an admirable woman of culture and refinement, who surrounded the youth and early manhood of
her child with a pure, disinterested love.
He pays a glowing tribute to her in a will
made about ten years before his death.

With the exception of a few hours a
day spent at a little country school, Taine's
early education was received in the bosom
of the family. Upon the untimely death
of his father, Mme. Taine's two brothers,
men of probity and character, assumed the

guardianship of the family. M. Adolphe Bezanson, the younger of the two, had lived for some years in the United States. He taught his nephew the English language, and it is to him that we are indebted, primarily, for one of Taine's masterpieces, "The History of English Literature," that incomparable gallery of portraits, in which the artist has combined, as it were, the genius and the technique of Albert Dürer and Meissonier.

Taine was not twenty when he wrote a sort of intellectual confession, in which he described the philosophic chaos that resulted from the undermining of his early religious opinions. He tells us that up to the age of fifteen he had lived in tranquil ignorance, with no thought of the future. He was a believing Christian, and the problems of existence had not even occurred to him. Suddenly reason flamed up "like a beacon light," startling him into intellectual activity. He began to suspect that there was something beyond his pres-

ent mental horizon, and entered upon a
dilligent search. It was not long before
religious faith was undermined. From
that time, he tells us, reason alone became
the *primum mobile* of his life.

Then came three years of discovery and
freedom, a period of happiness and intellectual adventure upon the unexplored
ocean of knowledge. Modern history and
even antiquity were ransacked; he found
himself the heir of an immense intellectual
inheritance. He felt the delight of ex-
changing existence under a dome of lead
for life in the boundless universe. He
read Guizot's lectures on "European Civi-
lization." This work, he says, "was like
a revelation." He began to search for
the general laws of history, and, with "the
inexperience and audacious confidence" of
youth, to attack questions that can only
be treated by men of ripe experience. In
spite of the loss of Christianity, he held to
belief in God, the immortality of the soul,
and the law of duty; but when he exam-

TAINE

ined the foundations and bulwarks of these
beliefs, he found that they were not im-
pregnable to the assaults of skepticism.
The day came when he found himself
drifting, hopeless and helpless, on the
shoreless seas of absolute infidelity. He
tells us, however, that he felt a certain
pride and joy in all this shipwreck. "I
exulted in the havoc I had made; I rev-
eled in exercising my intellect against the
opinions of the vulgar. I thought myself superior to those who believed. I
continued to advance until one day I found
that I had left nothing standing."

Then came sadness. He had been
wounded in what he held dearest, and had
blasphemed against the authority of the
intellect itself, hitherto enthroned by him
in the highest place. He felt lost, engulfed
in a kind of void. In these days of mental
despair, youth and health came to the
rescue. One is tempted to believe that the
period of storm and stress of the youthful
Taine, told with great interest in the ear-

lier letters, was not the martyrdom that it might have been for a more ardent and naïve nature. His description of these days of moral crisis leaves us as cold as one of his psychological reflections. This account of this life crisis is almost as soulless as his observations on Love: "I had an ardent love of Science and Art, of the True and the Beautiful. I felt capable of great efforts, of tenacious perseverance, had I but an object to attain, a design to fulfil. I felt a passionate admiration in the presence of beautiful things, especially the beauties of nature; and I suffered when I thought that I did not know how to make use of all this ardor and strength. Besides I was master of myself. I had accustomed my body and my soul to obey my will; and I had thus preserved myself from those bestial passions which blind and bewilder man, lure him from the study of his destiny, and lower him to the plane of the animal, which is ignorant of the present and careless of the future."

TAINE

Up to now his mind was virgin to all the philosophies. His skepticism was original, not suggested, as is ordinarily the case. The time had now arrived for a systematic training in the science of sciences. He found in philosophers nothing but contradictions, doubt and obscurity. Their reasoning seemed either puerile or incomprehensible. His clear and logical intellect pierced through their elaborate systems and left them in collapse. He was attracted toward Pantheism, which, tho old as thought itself, seemed new to him. Pantheism, usually the lure to destruction, was for Taine the plank of safety: "When tired of contradictions, I placed my mind at the service of the newest and most poetical idea—I supported Pantheism with all my heart. . . . This was my salvation, for from that moment Metaphysics appeared to me intelligible and science seemed serious."

On the wings of this system he soared out of the mists of doubt and attained the clear empyrean from whence he was enabled to survey the whole of the philosophical horizon. Spinoza's doctrine was "the ladder reaching heaven, and bright with beckoning angels."

Doubtless, as Renan says, the most interesting period of great men is their youth, for it is then that we seem to see through a veil their future stretching before them. It will be interesting to record the opinions of three distinguished Frenchmen who helped to form the youthful Taine at the École Normale.

"M. Taine has a remarkable intellect," said Jules Simon, "and he will sooner or later do credit to the École by publications of a serious order."

M. Saisset's report was as follows: "M. Taine unfolded in his lectures a clear, supple, resourceful mind, perfectly gifted for teaching. In written dissertation M. Taine is again in the front rank by the number and merit of his works. His principal defect is his excessive taste for the abstract.

TAINE

M. Taine should be encouraged and held
in check. He is the hope of the coming
competition."

M. Vacherot's estimate was remarkable
and prophetic:

"The hardest worker, the most remarkable student whom I have ever known at
the École Normale. Prodigiously learned
for his age. He has an ardor, an avidity
for knowledge, the like of which I have
never met with. A mind remarkable for
rapidity of conception, subtlety, delicacy,
and force of thought. Understands, con-
ceives, judges, and formulates too hastily,
however; is too fond of formulæ and defi-
nitions, to which he too often sacrifices
reality, quite unconsciously, however, for
he is perfectly sincere. Taine will make a
very distinguished professor, and will become a savant of the first order. With
great gentleness of character and amiable
manners, he has an indomitable firmness
of mind, so much so that no one exerts any
influence upon his thoughts. Indeed, he

27

is not of this world. Spinoza's motto will be his: 'Live to think.' Behavior and conduct excellent. As regards his morals, I believe his exceptional and superior nature is a stranger to every passion save the passion for Truth. This student easily stands first in all the examinations."

Let us now study at closer range the personality of the youthful Taine as it is revealed in his letters to his intimate friend, Prevost-Paradol. He confesses that the love of scenery is more to him than the love of woman. He has but little sympathy with his kind, and confesses that he takes no interest in the political and humanitarian ideas which are burning in the veins of the youth of that pregnant age. He seems absolutely devoid of generous and deep emotions. In these intimate outpourings to his college friend, in which he is endeavoring to warm himself at the fire of sentiment, the reader is hardly more moved than by a problem of geometry. He says, himself, that if he has

a unique passion it is for exactness. And
at twenty it is by *mathematical proofs* that
he convinces himself of the existence of
God!

At twenty-four, and without a thought
of adopting the medical profession, we find
him attending a course in anatomy and
physiology at the School of Medicine in
Paris. "That population of students and
professors is curious and their dissections
interesting. Butchers and scientists, what
devotion is theirs to Man, and what contempt! On the first day, with my spiritual
training, I was absolutely dumfounded,
but I had not a moment of disgust. Those
laws which repeat the same organs, in the
same places in all bodies, are magnificent.
The muscles of a young woman's back are
now being dissected in our presence. It
is a terrible and grandiose thought, that
of Nature, the eternal somnambulist.
What prodigality in her genius, and how
dead it all is! Ah, my poor Cartesians!"[1]

---

[1] From a letter to Eduard de Suckau.

BALZAC—A CRITICAL STUDY

These lines reveal him as in a flashlight photograph. We see him in his element. In the same letter he tells his friend that he employs *his leisure* in reading Esquirol on mental diseases. He is deeply interested in those seances of the operating table, and as usual regards the scene with the eye and introspection of a philosopher. The doctors and students are a poor lot in his opinion. They are "skeptical sawbones." It is at this time that he begins to sketch what is afterward to be elaborated into one of the masterpieces of modern thought, the work on "Intelligence."

Even first love is a subject for disdain and philosophizing. He uses Cupid's dart as tho it were a scalpel. At the age when pure-hearted and romantic youth catches its glimpse of the ideal in the Paradise of first love, he is constructing syllogisms upon the master passion. We are reminded of Napoleon's remark that if he even happened to fall in love, his principal interest in the love-making would be

30

to analyze the emotion psychologically. Listen to Taine at twenty-one, recording his ideas upon the passion that "makes Heaven drowsy with its harmonies:"

"Love is a faculty and not a need; true love is sufficient unto itself, and, like thought, happy in its own activity; it is devoted, it is not monopolistic nor destructive like sensual or covetous passion; it does not aspire to make of the beloved object a mere appendage of itself; it does not consider itself in what it feels and accomplishes for the beloved object; but it lives in the object, and thus duplicates its own existence. It is the perfect preservation of two personalities in the absolute union of two beings; it is not selfish or jealous; it suffers that the beloved object should love others; it has but one object, which is to become more united, and to make the loved one more perfect; it is like a sculptor, who, his eyes fixed on the ideal model, corrects and embellishes his divine statues day by day. It is not languid, dreamy, melancholy, tearful; it is strong, sensible, reasonable, courageous; it is not a passion but an activity. Man is not possessed, mastered, or lessened by it; through its means he is strengthened, exalted, and made divine, as he is by the assiduous exercise of thought and action."

The binomial theorem is not more sober nor more exact. It is easy to believe in Taine's stock of virtue after reading this effusion. Diana's priest is not colder. A surgeon who should attempt a sonnet in the intervals of an operation would achieve a finer thrill. We have read with attention the whole of Taine's intimate correspondence without experiencing the shadow of emotion. This utter subjugation of the heart by the head, this supreme domination of intellect over the natural emotional faculties, is probably unique in the history of modern men of letters. This temperamental coldness, this ruthless attitude of the operating room and lack of human sympathy which would be fatal in the case

of the ordinary writer, is, however, one
of the secrets of Taine's power. For his
lack of warmth and human sympathy are
atoned for by the clairvoyance of his
thought. He seems to have lived the life
of an ascetic, and the crystal-clearness of
his ideas and conceptions are wholly un-
moved by passion. It is to these qualities
that the world owes the work on "Intelligence" and the invaluable "Origins of
Contemporary France."

For a mind of this order there are no
enthusiasms and no idolatries. We are at
the other pole from Carlyle's hero wor-
ship. In the infinite and complicated
scheme of things governed by iron laws,
fatally interrelated, and interdependent,
there are no exceptions. Cromwell, Robespierre, and Napoleon do not appear as
isolated phenomena. Monotheism, Christianity, Islam, the French Revolution, the
new modern philosophical conception—
Evolution, are not extraordinary and isolated facts. They are the result of fatal

laws. Hobbes was not more implacable than the French determinist in his attempt to bring everything in the universe under the yoke of iron law. The conquest which this system of fatal determinism is to achieve over the mind of Taine is adumbrated from his early years. His schoolboy professions of love for Platonic and Pantheistic systems were like most first loves—ephemeral. His early soarings were merely Icarian flights. The concrete wonders of the laboratory, the amazing revelations of physical science, will completely transform the metaphysical system of his earlier allegiance. His name will become the battle-cry of those who have proclaimed war upon the spiritual, and comparatively early in his career he will be denounced by the Church.

Taine is revealed, as in a lightning flash, by a celebrated phrase which he once used: "Vice and virtue are products like vitriol or sugar." That phrase sounded like a defiance, and it was interpreted as the

watchword of Atheism by orthodox opinion in France. It was uttered without
thought of giving offense, and as the simple condensed expression of the ethics of
a convinced materialist. For a time practically the whole thinking world was
leagued against him, and his scientific
theories were denounced as the rankest
heresy.

What a gulf yawns between the maker
of this epigram and the philosopher of the
student days who had written this to his
friend, Prevost-Paradol: "I lay great
stress upon this question of the existence
and nature of God, because it is in reality
the only question in philosophy. . . .
If you wish to know the Beautiful, the
Good, the True, if you wish to prove that
there is a law of conduct for man, an im-
mutable goal for the artist, an absolute
certainty for the scientist, you will be
obliged to examine into the nature of God
and to believe in Him."

The definitive phase of Taine's philosophy is stark materialism. He became a partisan who gave no quarter. Holding to an inexorable determinism, he declared war upon the spiritual ideas, which, in 1845, began to dawn in France. These ideas positively maddened him. He proclaimed that knowledge was impossible except through sensations, transferred by means of abstraction into ideas. His final word was "Metaphysics does not exist." Observe what kind of an impression Taine's philosophy makes upon a typically modern idealist. Amiel says:

"In reading him I have a painful sensation—something like the grinding of pulleys, the click of machines, the smell of the laboratory. His style reeks of chemistry and technology; it is inexorably scientific. It is dry and rigid, hard and penetrating, a strong astringent; it lacks charm, humanity, nobleness, and grace. It sets one's ears tingling and one's teeth on edge. This painful sensation probably comes from two things, his moral philosophy and his liter-

36

ary method. The profound contempt for humanity which characterizes the physiological school, and the intrusion of technology into literature, inaugurated by Balzac and Stendhal, explain this latest aridity which you feel in his pages, and which catches you in the throat like the fumes of a mineral factory. He is very instructive to read, but he takes the life out of you; he parches, corrodes, and saddens you. He never inspires, he only informs. This, I suppose, is to be the literature of the future, an Americanized literature, in profound contrast with the Greek; giving you algebra in place of life, the formula instead of the image, the fumes of the alembic instead of the divine intoxication of Apollo, the cold demonstration for the joys of thought—in a word, the immolation of the ideal, a poetry skinned and dissected by science."

Conceptions in the higher regions of metaphysics are restricted to a certain order of minds. It is a fact of much in-

terest that to many persons, by no means
deficient in intellect, a metaphysical con-
cept presents itself in the light of an absurdity. Very often men with a special
aptitude for material science are incapable
of comprehending the simplest metaphysical idea. Herbert Spencer, in his recently
published autobiography makes the astonishing statement that Kant's doctrine of
Time and Space remained for him an absurdity throughout his life. He admits
his sheer inability to understand the "Critique of Pure Reason." If a mind of Spencer's capacity betrayed a lack in this domain, is it not possible that Taine may
have been equally deficient? The two men
were singularly alike in their grasp of reality, and their systems of thought have
many points of resemblance.

What Taine possessed was a construct-
ive imagination. He was denied the rarest gift. This is the reason that his letters
and his personality are rather uninterest-
ing, while his scientific and literary pro-

ductions vibrate with interest. The descriptions of natural scenery which abound in his works, and his descriptions in general, are often catalogs, and sometimes tiresome catalogs. They bear the same relation to real and poetical description that a photograph bears to a painting. The immense range of his learning had supplied him with a vocabulary of astonishing opulence, and this, used to advantage and coupled with a striking and bizarre manner of antithesis and poignant metaphors, give an original distinction to his style. This style, powerful at times, but often meretricious, has provoked severe criticism. Compared to the purity and clear beauty of the prose of Renan, it becomes unendurable. It is as tho we were to compare the Acropolis to a modern skyscraper.

His scenery is not nature; it is a herbarium lit by electricity. The magic, the sorcery of words, that indefinable, subtle, and inspiring essence which is the soul of poetry and which lies beyond the reaches of chemistry, is non-existent in Taine. Hence a notable dryness characterizes some of his work.

In spite of his lack of the poetic faculty, however, he is able to astonish us at will by his brilliant paradox and wizardry of words. Certain passages remind us of a brightly uniformed army marching with streaming banners and glittering bayonets to the strains of martial music. We hear the blare of trumpets and watch with a certain admiration the glittering phalanxes moving in ordered files and exhibiting different maneuvers.

The unique and extraordinary influence which Taine acquired over the thought of contemporary Europe was, nevertheless, due to no factitious circumstance, to no tricks of style. It was the result of vast intellectual labors pursued with a Spartan severity from early youth onward through a long life. When hardly more than a boy he had solemnly "dedicated himself upon the altars of knowledge," and vowed to spend his life in the pursuit of truth. His devotion to science has somewhat the character of the medieval ascetic. It is a kind of holy enthusiasm far removed from passion and devoid of all trace of human tenderness. The divinity to whom he yields homage is the God of pure intellect.

This Trappist of science presents a striking contrast with his famous contemporary and friend, Renan. Poetic charm, human sympathy, spiritual imagination, the beauty and purity of style, the inimitable and subtle graces of creative literary art, which were the endowment of the most brilliant of the thinkers of modern France, were wholly lacking in Taine. They were even despised by him. His intellectual armament was of a wholly different caliber.

Paul Bourget has given us an inimitable sketch of Taine as he appeared to his pupils:

"The master spoke in a slightly monotonous tone, and there was a vague foreign accent in his words, uttered in short phrases; and yet this very monotony, these rare gestures, that absorbed physiognomy, that extreme care lest he should add factitious eloquence to the real eloquence of the documents—all these details exerted over us a species of seduction. This man, so modest that he seemed to have no suspicion of his European reputation, and of such simplicity that his only care seemed to be to serve truth, became for us the apostle of the New Faith. Here, at least, was one who had never sacrificed at the altar of the official doctrine. Here was a man who had never lied. These little phrases, so terse, so full of meaning, contained his real ideas—ideas of a thorough and invincible sincerity."

II

IT is difficult to realize the passionate earnestness that fired the intellectual life of the generation of Taine. It was an epoch of freedom and discovery. In the wake of the French Revolution, which had effected political emancipation, came the movement for the enfranchisement of mind. Modern science had dawned on the world. Kant, the herald of that dawn, had opened to mankind intellectual vistas of unexampled originality, and his countrymen were pushing their conquests farther into the realm of the unknown. In Germany, comparative philology had effected an independent revolution in theological thought—a revolution whose consequences were destined to be profound and far-reaching, and the ultimate fruits

43

of which have only begun to be garnered in our own day.

But by far the most important of these epoch-making events were the doctrines associated with the name of Darwin, which at this time were given to the world. At the present time, when theological ideas receive scant consideration among men of science, it is difficult to realize the earthquake shock which the theory of Evolution effected in the orthodox camp. Nor is it easy to realize the strength of inspiration which the new theory produced in minds like Taine. The youthful and emancipated intellect of France yearned toward the new ideals with a fervor akin to religion. It was a period of grandiose dreams and ambitions. It was the intellectual counterpart of the great epoch which had witnessed the discovery of new continents. Men ventured boldly upon unmapped seas, and one of these daring voyagers of the Ideal had found a new world.

TAINE

Foremost among the young paladins of progress was Taine, who in time became their representative and champion. This movement is found in its most developed form toward 1850. It is seen not only in literature, but in the plastic arts as well, and is recognized in a striving for reality and objective truth. It was a protest against the romantic movement which had ended in bankruptcy. Its best representatives in the field of the novel are perhaps Flaubert and Zola. Its influence is felt perceptibly in history and philosophy. A spirit of intense materialism pervades thought. A taste for mathematics, natural history, physiology, psychology, philology, reveals itself among the learned. A determination to arrive at truth by more exact methods than those hitherto employed is the distinguishing characteristic in every department of thought. This movement did not come spontaneously. It had been prepared by the writings of Stendhal, Balzac, Sainte-Beuve, and Auguste Comte. By the middle of the century it was the recognized principle of intellectual life in France. Like every new doctrine, this movement of scientific realism, as it may be called, produced an extraordinary wave of enthusiasm, and, as is usually the case, many of the ancient landmarks and moorings were swept away. Some of the ablest minds of Europe were caught in the current of materialism.

Taine's famous theory that great men are the product of "race epoch and environment," applies with singular accuracy to himself. He is typical of his country and his race. In him the distinctive French traits attain complete development. Harmonious simplicity, an intuitive faculty almost equal to clairvoyance, an utter absence of mysticism, are now his dominant traits. Naturally he has the defects of his qualities, and his genius for comprehending facts and arranging them into coordinate systems, his unrivaled skill in

46

generalizing, are at the cost of certain magnetic qualities which we expect in a writer.

The famous theory of the influence of climate and environment upon human character had been formulated by Montesquieu and Stendhal, but in Taine's hands it underwent such development, and was carried to such perfection, as to constitute an original creation. This theory of the influence of environment upon human character colors deeply the entire work of Taine. It is wrought out with much elaboration in his "History of English Literature," and it plays the chief rôle in all his historical and literary studies.

Taine's philosophical system, he tells us, was largely influenced by Hegel, for whom, strangely enough, he had an intense admiration. He once declared that the principal task of contemporary philosophers is to "re-think" the ideas of the famous German metaphysician: "They (Hegel's ideas) may be reduced to a single one: development (*Entwickelung*), which consists in representing all the constituents of a group as solidary and complementary, in such fashion that each one necessitates the rest, and that when reunited they manifest by their successive series and contrasts the eternal quality which brings them together and produces them." This identical quality, which Hegel calls the *idea,* becomes for Taine the "dominating fact." The vague metaphysical formulas of the German metaphysician crystalize in the crucible of the Frenchman.

It is difficult to trace any real resemblance between the German somnambulist of thought and the keen and practical Frenchman whose final declaration was, as we have seen, "metaphysics does not exist;" but Taine has more than once insisted on his debt to Hegel, and it is at least probable that his talent for organization was aided by his study of that philosopher.

TAINE

Any adequate account of Taine's system is, of course, out of the question here, but it may be permissible, perhaps, to glance at the famous theory of "race environment and epoch," without some understanding of which it is impossible to appreciate Taine at all. And this may be done without risk of being tiresome by considering the theory in its relation to his celebrated "History of English Literature."

Taine, himself, tells us that it was his ambition to write the history of a literature and to investigate the psychology of a people. In order to accomplish this task adequately it was necessary to select a complete literature. Latin literature is largely an imitation, German literature lacks continuity, the literature of Italy and Spain come to an end in the middle of the seventeenth century. There remained ancient Greece and modern France and England.

It was for weighty reasons that the historian fixed his choice upon England. The literature of that country, he declares, presents a continuous development, and its varied epochs teem with dramatic episodes full of interest for the critical investigator. This vast unexplored region, rich in life and color, was almost ideally adapted to the purposes of Taine, and he entered upon his task with the vigor and enthusiasm of a discoverer. The immense field which lay before him was almost virgin. A history of English literature in the modern sense did not exist. So-called histories had been attempted, but they were superficial and without value as criticism. Taine ignored them utterly and entered upon his work under wholly original auspices. The result of his immense labors is not merely a brilliant record of literary epochs, but a history of the English people and character possessing incomparable interest and value.

For Taine a literary work is not a mere product of the imagination, it is a tran-

script of contemporary manners and the
symbol of a particular state of intelligence.
Works of literature are, therefore, historical monuments and the truest of all rec-
ords of the past. This truth, which had
already dawned upon Montesquieu and
Stendhal, arrived at its full development
in the hands of Taine, and its effect has
been completely to revolutionize historical
methods. According to this view a literary document, an ancient manuscript or
book, a poem, a code of laws, is simply a
mold on a fossil shell. Beneath the shell
there once existed an animal; behind the
document there lived a man. As an idea
of the animal may be had from the study
of the shell, so the man may be comprehended from a study of the document.
Both are dead fragments, whose chief
value is that they enable us to reconstruct
the living being. "True history," says
Taine, "begins when the historian has dis-
cerned beyond the mists of ages the living, active man, endowed with passions,

furnished with habits, special in voice, feature, gesture, and costume, distinctive and complete, like anybody that you have just encountered in the street." According to him a language, a law, a creed is never more than an abstraction. The real thing is to be sought in concrete form, in the living man.

The problem which Taine proposes for solution is this: A literature, philosophy, or society being given, what are the moral conditions which have produced it? What are the conditions of race, epoch, and environment, which are the best to bring about this moral state? Not only for the development of art in general, but for each particular art—for painting, sculpture, architecture, poetry, music—it is necessary that there be distinct moral conditions. Human development is never haphazard, but is the result of law.

"The great achievements of painting in Flanders in the seventeenth century, of poetry in England in the sixteenth cen-

TAINE

tury, of music in Germany in the eighteenth century, can be traced to the presence of certain germs, of certain psychological conditions. It is the laws of human
regulation for which history must now
search; it is this special psychology of each
special formation which must be got at.
There is nothing more delicate or more
difficult. Montesquieu undertook it, but
in his day the interest in history was too
recent to achieve success; nobody, indeed,
had any idea of the road that was to be
followed, and even at the present day we
are only beginning to obtain a glimpse of
it. Just as harmony at bottom is a mechanical problem, and physiology a chem-
ical problem, so history is at bottom a
problem of psychology. There is a particular system of inner impressions which
fashions the artist, the believer, the musi-
cian, the painter, the nomad, the social
man. . . . If a document is rich, and
we know how to interpret it, we shall find
in it the psychology of a particular soul,

53

often that of an age and sometimes that of a race. In this respect a great poem, a good novel, the confessions of a superior man are more instructive than a mass of historians and histories."

By race Taine means the innate hereditary dispositions and qualities of men and the accompanying difference of temperament and physical structure. "There are," he bluntly tells us, "varieties of men as there are varieties of cattle." Some are naturally brave and intelligent, others are timid and without capacity. Some are capable of elevated conceptions and creations; others are of limited ability. This racial force or characteristic is so strong that its influence is distinctly observable in the people throughout thirty centuries of revolutions, in spite of climatic changes and religious and political transformations. The parentage can be traced in spite of barbarism, culture-grafting, difference of soil or climate. The great characteristics of the original form

54

persist with fatal tenacity, and the leading features of the primitive stamp are apparent under the subsequent imprints received in the course of time or chance.

According to Taine there is nothing surprising in this extraordinary tenacity. Altho the immense distance of time enables us to catch a mere glimpse in the doubtful light of Darwin's theory of the origin of species, the events of history throw sufficient light on prehistoric events to prove the almost unshaken solidity of primordial traits. These traits encountered twenty or thirty centuries before our era in an Aryan, Chinese, or Egyptian, are the result of perhaps many thousands of centuries. The animal must adapt itself to its environment. Differences of climate and situation create different necessities: hence different activities and eventually a different system of habits, of aptitudes, of instincts. Man compelled to adapt himself to circumstances, contracts a corresponding character and temperament, "and

55

his character, like his temperament, are
acquisitions all the more stable because of
the outward impression being all the more
deeply imprinted in him by frequent rep-
etitions and transmitted to the offspring
by more ancient heredity.

"So that at each moment of time the
character of a people may be considered as
a summary of all antecedent actions and
sensations; that is to say as a quantity and
as a weighty mass, not infinite, since all
things in nature are limited, but disproportionate to the rest and almost impossible
to raise, since each minute of an almost
infinite past contributed to render it heav-
ier; and in order to turn the scale, it would
require on the other side a still greater
accumulation of actions and sensations.
Such is the first and most abundant source
of these master faculties from which historic events are derived; and we see at
once that if it is powerful it is owing to
its not being a mere source, but a sort of
lake, and as it is more a deep reservoir

wherein other sources have found their waters for a multitude of centuries."

Such, in scant outline, is the famous theory which was destined to leave so profound a stamp upon French and world literature. Tho found in germ, as has been intimated, in previous writers, it does not attain practical and formal development until it is adopted by Taine as the central dogma of his system. Presently, as I shall have occasion to point out at more length, it assumes portentous significance, as it passes from the domain of literature into that of politics.

III

In 1808, Napoleon, then near the zenith
of his power, founded the École Normale,
which he designed as a nursery for the
emancipated youth of France. It was the
Emperor's intention that the institution
should serve primarily to train young men
of superior minds for the teaching profession. And it is a striking instance of that
fatal irony which runs through history,
that in founding this beneficent institution
he was laying the axe at the root of his
future glory, for fifty years later there
issued full armed from this arsenal of
thought—Hippolyte Adolphe Taine.

While it is hazardous to predict the per-
manence of any renown, however exalted
by the admiration of contemporaries, it is
probable that Taine is destined to endur-

ing fame, and that that fame will rest upon a basis outside of his purely literary
achievement. Far more important than
the psychological revelations of "Intelligence," more fascinating than the "History of English Literature," more original than the theories of race and surroundings, is the remarkable monograph
on Napoleon, which constitutes about one-
third of "The Modern Régime." In the
library of literature that has grown round
the figure of the French emperor, there
is nothing to compare with that. The
time may come when Taine's theories will
be as obsolete as are those of Descartes,
which in their day had an equal vogue.
It is even conceivable that the greater part
of "The Origins of Contemporary France"
may go the way of dusty death. But what
seems absolutely impossible is that pos-
terity will ever lose interest in Taine's portrait of Napoleon Bonaparte.

What gives Taine unique distinction
among the learned men of his time, is the

fact that his writings have exerted an important practical influence upon political events in France. What gives him an unrivaled place in a group of thinkers rarely equaled in a single generation, is the fact that his ideas have actually altered the current of French history. Taine's profound studies in history, illuminated by the apparatus of modern scientific criticism which he invented, convinced him that the political malady of his country, culminating in the frightful crisis of 1870, was due to a false principle which had been assimilated by the nation. He believed that the great Italian whose supreme genius still obsessed the French people, had, in reality, done them mortal injury by seducing them into paths which led into the past instead of toward the future. In his view Napoleonic imperialism was a survival rather than progress, and he believed that until the taint of the Napoleonic virus was extirpated from the blood of Frenchmen, there could be no real advancement. This

idea, which in time took complete possession of Taine, is the soul of the "Origins
of Contemporary France." The literary
recluse, the dreamer of metaphysical
dreams, had become an active political
propagandist, and his motto was a portentous one: *"Écrasez l'infâme!"*

Let us look for a moment at the mag-
nitude of the undertaking that he set
himself to accomplish, single-handed. Up
to the time of Taine the name and memory of Napoleon had exerted a species of
sorcery over France. The halo of splendor was rather enhanced than diminished
by the bastard purple and sham empire of
Louis Napoleon, and not even the shame
and disgrace of 1870 could uproot from
the hearts of Frenchmen the inherited
idolatry of the great Emperor. The
dizzy eminence of that fame had made
criticism puerile. The spectacle of the
antique Cæsar become incarnate in France
at the definitive epoch of human enlight-
enment, the apotheosis of the people in his

person, the established humiliation of the royalty and aristocracy of Europe, the flood of splendor which the genius of this incomparable Italian had shed over France —all seemed to make his fame secure.

Up to the time of Taine that career had baffled criticism. Against the background of modern history loomed the figure of the Man of Destiny, original, dazzling, and incomparable. That personality, surrounded by national idolatry, had become almost august. Seen in the luminous haze of history, it had assumed gigantic proportions. It imposed upon history. Victor Hugo said of Napoleon: "He was a hindrance to God."

Taine found himself confronted with a problem of startling proportions. How was it brought about that an outcast foreigner, flung by fate into the whirlpool of the French Revolution, had arrived at the hegemony of Europe? How account for this unheard of miracle, a hungry Corsican breathing the spirit of invincibility

into a ragged army, conquering the civil-
ized portions of the world, and bringing
the fabric of European monarchy to earth
with a thrust of his sword? How explain
the fact that in the wake of the most extraordinary democratic upheaval in history, with the echoes of crashing. mon-
archies still ringing in the ears of Paris,
at a period when the bloody wraiths of
Robespierre, Danton and Marat had
hardly fainted off from the horizon—how
explain the fact that this man was able to
roll back the tide of the Revolution, and on
the ruins of the costly popular liberties
erect a personal despotism that in modern
times realized the dream of the first Cæsar? How explain the bewildering accom-
plished fact of Charlemagne renascent in
the Nineteenth Century? How account
for the phenomenon of an antique hero
fronting the age of steam and annulling
the Philosophy of History?

Such was the problem, desperate
enough seemingly, that Tain set himself

to unriddle; and he began by inquiring into the racial origins of Napoleon. The antique beauty of that personality had not escaped the admiration of man. But the identification of Napoleon with the unique and masterful species enrooted originally in the soil of Italy, had been merely fanciful. In the original mind of Taine it assumed reality. It remained for this penetrating, critical intellect to perceive the astonishing, tho natural enough, fact that this son of Italian Corsica, who held Europe in his iron grip in the nineteenth century, was the lineal descendant of the Cæsars, the Sforzas, and the Borgias, of the mighty condottieri of the Renaissance. There was nothing French in this idol of France. This mind and personality, cast in the antique mold, were entirely out of harmony with modern ideals. By heredity, by right and logically there descended to that head with the Roman profile, the diadem of the Cæsars.

It was Tain with his scientific insight,

and his marvelous apparatus of modern criticism, who penetrated to the heart of the mystery. Focussed in the reflecting telescope of Taine, the figure of the Titan emerges from its haze of legend, and stands revealed as one of the rarest types in Nature's laboratory, but a type entirely explicable by scientific criticism. We are brought face to face with the last scion of the mother of empires; we recognize the latest descendant of the Mistress of the World. As scene by scene is unfolded, we are enabled for the first time to study that unequalled career under the blaze of the searchlight of science. Suddenly there dawns for us a new conception of Napoleon, startling, disillusionizing, and terrible.

The disillusionment is complete. The white light of science has dissipated the mists of legend. Stripped of the purple glories and of the factitious honors lavished by an enthusiastic people, Napoleon looms as the modern incarnation of ferocious Italian egotism,—ruthless, implacable, unfeeling, and pitiless, hard as flint, merciless as fate. We become aware for the first time of a unique species of intellect, unparagoned in history, and produced in one soil only—Italy. We recognize the characteristics of the mighty figures, whose blood-red nimbus illumines the dark background of the Renaissance. We see clearly in Bonaparte the full brother of Cæsar Borgia, and we remember that the son of Pope Alexander VI. was obsessed by the same grandoise vanity and colossal ambition. We trace the identical characteristics of glory, pride, sensuality, unbridled passion, ambition verging on insanity, superhuman courage, and the indomitable will that break through all obstacles and defy all moral laws.

Taine shows conclusively that in Napoleon we are confronted with a survival of that insatiable Italian egotism that throws so lurid a charm over the despots of the sixteenth century. He points

out that the rare species had appeared
before upon the stage of History, but that,
hitherto, the theater had been inadequate.
At last all was prepared, the man and the
hour had arrived: and what the world
then witnessed, and history has since stood
aghast at, was simply the working out of
natural laws when an intellect of supreme
force and originality imposes itself upon
a nation in the throes of political transformation. Taine has shown clearly and
irrefutably that absolute egotism was the
basis of Napoleon's character and that
his unexampled triumph was at the cost
of all that mankind holds dear. Personal
glory, self agrandizement, the gratification of a measureless ambition, are shown
to be the mainspring of his acts. Taine
exhibits him as the supreme artist of history, producing an unexampled masterpiece; only, instead of marble his chisel
is at work upon the sensitive flesh of
humanity.

Look well upon this formidable drypoint etching of "the man without a model and without a shadow," for in the long portrait gallery of history from Plutarch to Carlyle there is nothing to compare with it. Taine has mounted, for a moment, to the level of Michæl Angelo and Dante, and like those masters, has painted against the somber background of the evil-ideal, a portrait of incomparable grandeur.

The fearful arraignment of the national idol provoked deep resentment. Prince Jerome Napoleon, himself a distinguished scientist and admirer of Taine's genius, was stung to bitter retort. He denounced the critic as an entomologist examining fragments of anatomy under the microscope, and oblivious of the meaning and the beauty of the whole. Taine ignored the public clamor, merely remarking to a friend that time would vindicate his judgment. The prophecy has already been realized. Since his time the Napoleonic legend has ceased to be a menace to the peace of France. The malignant

TAINE

taint of Bonapartism, which was a perpetual menace to the French Republic, has been effectually cauterized by the iron pen of the great materialist historian.

In spite of the comparative reticence of his published correspondence, and of the thick veil that shrouds his personality, let us endeavor to arrive at some intimate knowledge of this great Frenchman, whose work has left so profound an impression upon contemporary thought. There are extant at least two portraits of Taine. One shows him in vigorous maturity, the other in old age. The earlier portrait is that of a full-bearded man of clear-cut features, with full head of hair, combed in rather severe fashion, respectably commonplace to the last degree. It is a type we meet with every day. This picture suggests a cold, dignified, unsympathetic temperament; it might be the face of a successful jurist or physician.

69

There is some distinction in the face but no gleam of genius.

In the older portrait time has wrought transformations. The hair and beard have become scanty and gray, and the originally hard lines now convey a suggestion of the pessimism that marked his later writings. The face distinctly lacks amiability. The expression denotes an intelligence that retains its pristine vigor; the eyes are clear but contracted with that expression of intensity so often noticed in the scientist whose life has become a passion and a search for tangible facts. For the student of Taine this portrait has far more interest than the other. What it expresses is the very negation of the ideal. We do not wonder now that the mind of which this face is the index, proclaimed the dogma: "Metaphysics does not exist," nor are we surprised at the statement that the philosophy of the idealist school produced in him a kind of loathing. We catch a glimpse of a species of mind which had its counterpart in d'Holbach and the atheists of the eighteenth century, men whose philosophy depends upon the scalpel and the melting pot. In this portrait there is no suggestion of the enthusiastic philosopher of the youthful letters who, for a brief moment, was lifted into the empyrean of Plato and Spinoza. This is the face of a man completely disillusionized and pessimistic, whose chief interest in the human species is that it provides specimens for his surgeon's knife and microscope. What we see revealed in this picture is a cold and unimpressionable nature. We remember that Taine had an innate dislike for the society of his fellow creatures, and we recall that his youthful letters are filled with unamiable remarks at the expense of the pupils whom necessity forced upon him.

From the fact that Taine, like most Frenchmen, was born and reared in the Roman Catholic faith—a creed which he abandoned early in his career—one would naturally expect in him some signs of lingering affection for the faith of his fathers. Nothing of this kind, however, appears in his works or letters. Whatever sparks of religion are possible to his flinty nature are struck out by Protestantism, for which system, strangely enough in a man of his caliber, he seems to have had great respect. For Catholicism he had that dislike peculiar to materialistic minds, for whom the most venerable of religious systems is logically defective, and who are blinded by their nature to its moral and historic grandeur. This does not imply that he had the bad taste to insult the religion of his childhood. On the contrary, in "The Modern Régime" he demonstrates the absolute necessity to the French people of the historic creed, so ruthlessly extirpated by Jacobin stupidity; but there is no note of a faith loved tho lost, such as we find in the pages of Renan.

Characteristically, he had a penchant for asking questions, and it was remarked that to be cross-questioned by Taine was more instructive than to be lectured by other professors. His curiosity was insatiable and amounted to a passion. To it must be ascribed the interesting quality of his writings, for this taste prompted him to investigations of a colossal character. Whole libraries were ransacked for the material of a few chapters of the "Origins." He took nothing for granted, and the word "perhaps" is rarely found in his writings. Paul Bourget once remarked that he bore a striking resemblance to that character in Dickens who exhibited such a notable predilection for "facts."

While engaged in the colossal task of the "Origins," Taine had occasion to ascertain the actual number of communicants in France. The method he adopted was novel and certainly characteristic. He made a visit to a certain manufacturer of wafers in Paris and asked him *how many he had sold during a certain number of years.* He reasoned that by computing the increase or falling off in the demand for consecrated wafers he might calculate with absolute exactness to what extent practical religion was waxing or waning in France.

By a paradox not unusual, Taine's pessimist conception of life had no effect upon his intercourse with the relatively few persons admitted to his intimacy. With all he was invariably kind, courteous, considerate and modest. He gave himself no airs of greatness. He was simple, candid, even childlike in the ordinary intercourse of family life. One day a visitor, tempted to curiosity by the far-reaching fame of the author of "The Origins of Contemporary France," called to see the great man. Expectant of some of the pomp and circumstance of greatness, the visitor was somewhat dashed by the reality. When ushered into the presence of Taine he saw him sitting on the floor, all his energies, mental and physical, bent to the task of putting on his little grandson's shoes. "You must excuse me," said the philosopher, "he absolutely refuses to allow anybody but me to put them on."

It is a strange commentary upon the unfathomable paradox of human nature, that this Grand Inquisitor of History was in the ordinary intercourse of life merciful, indulgent, conservative, even sympathetic. The man who outrivaled Carlyle's remark about the majority of men being mostly fools, by the more bitter one that a considerable portion of the race are "simply noxious animals," was far from being malevolent in his personal relation with his kind. His profound researches in universal history had, however, given him a low opinion of human nature. This pessimism was confirmed and deepened by the fiendish events of the Commune. The abyss of human depravity which opened before his eyes in 1870 seems to have left sinister shadows which tinged all his subsequent writings. He had beheld with his own eyes what the human animal is capable of when having slipped the leash of law, the primeval passions reassert their sway.

His materialism was due to a funda-- mental trait of his hard, uncompromising, practical character. It is difficult to avoid the conclusion that the youthful professions of love for philosophy, made in the letters of his student period, were due to a certain collegian vanity rather than to any natural or profound impulse. The only department of philosophy which held his interest was psychology, and this continued to fascinate him to the last, especially in its practical aspect, and probably by reason of its adaptability to experiment. He tells us in his letters that from his youth onward it was his custom to analyze and study minutely all his sensations, and carefully to write down the results of his meditations. It seems that he had a taste for music, and true to his instincts, he was fascinated by the most artificial of musical

TAINE

instruments—the piano. He became a
fairly good performer, and was wont to
vary the monotony of his intellectual dissections by experimenting with chords
and harmonious combinations.

It will be observed that no matter what
phase of his genius be examined, what
stands out most prominently is his *mechanical instinct,* if one may use such an
expression. Some idea of this may, perhaps, be obtained from the following ex-
tract taken from the final chapter of "The
Classic Philosophers of the Nineteenth
Century," which contains, in remarkable
condensation, the philosophy of Taine:

"We confine ourselves within the region
of facts; we have drawn upon no metaphysical entity; our only design has been
to constitute groups. These groups being
given, we have replaced them by the generating fact. We have represented this
fact by a formula. We have reunited the
different formulas into a group, and we
have sought for the superior fact which

has engendered them. We have continued thus and have arrived at last at a unique fact which is the universal cause. In calling it the cause we have simply meant that from its formula may be deduced all the others, and all that follows from the others. We have thus transformed the scattered multitude of facts into a hierarchy of propositions, of which the first, a universal, creative power, engenders a group of subordinated propositions, which, in time, produce each a new group, and this in series up to the point when there appear the multiplied details and the particular facts of sensible observation."

Advertence has been made to the incident which led Taine to the study of the English language. Drinking deeply at the rich, sparkling fountains of English literature seems to have had a reviving influence upon a nature too deeply saturated with science, and the "hard brassy"

style undergoes an alchemy that trans-
mutes it into pure gold The fascination
thus exerted upon him is attested by his
work in four volumes, "The History of
English Literature." This work is known
throughout the world, and has made its
author's name famous in English speaking
countries. It is the most valuable compen-
dium of the kind that exists, and has been
an unfailing sourse of delight and inspiration to countless students. That such a
book should have been produced by a
Frenchman is one of the miracles of literature. No work by an English writer
on the same subject can be compared with
it. Tho not free from defects, which have
been dwelt upon with great interest by
English critics, who can not forgive a
Frenchman for having beaten them upon
their own ground, the work comes very
close to being a definitive history of the
epochs and figures of this incomparable
literature.

In this, as in his other historical studies,

Taine has brought to bear his enormous erudition and unrivaled psychological and critical equipment. The result is a panorama of an immense period, amazing and intensely interesting—a series of pastels of striking brilliance, studded with gems borrowed from the masters, and enriched with enchanting landscapes and charming figures. This panorama is unfolded in ordered scenes, revealing "the cloud-capped towers, the gorgeous palaces" of Shakespeare, the broad, golden rivers of Milton, the splendors of the English Renaissance, the finished landscape gardens of the classic period, with glimpses of Pope and Swift and Bolingbroke. In time there appears upon the scene Byron, heir of the great line of English poets; and lastly Tennyson, one of the noblest of the line, lacking the seer's madness of Shakespeare, but inheriting his lyric sweetness, and adding to the poet's golden visions rich stores of modern science, the softened evening phase of the far-flaming sun of Shakespeare.

TAINE

Taine spent twenty years of labor upon his master work, "The Origins of Contemporary France." It was while putting the final touches upon this edifice that the hand of death was laid gently upon the tireless builder, so that unfortunately a column or an architrave will here or there be found wanting. This work will probably be the test of Taine's future fame. It is unlike all other histories, is wonderfully accurate in its facts, and whatever may be thought of the peculiar philosophical doctrines upon which its main thesis rests, it has been acclaimed as an important contribution to modern history.

As regards Taine's place in literature, there have been much discussion and difference of opinion among professional critics. Saintsbury distinctly denies him greatness, and critics have even gone the length of writing the word, charlatan, across his fame. Probably the fairest criticism, one with which many will be inclined to agree, is that of Ferdinand

BALZAC—A CRITICAL STUDY

Brunetière. This eminent authority, while not agreeing with Taine's scientific dogmatism concerning the absolute influence of race and climate on character and mind, yet pays a remarkable tribute to "the real beauty of his work—a beauty learned, austere, somewhat laborious, perhaps, but solid and durable." He testifies to "the grandeur and vigorous originality of Taine's work," and declares that since Hegel no writer in Europe has put into circulation so many new and profound ideas. This tribute of the learned academician is highly significant from the fact that he is regarded as in some sense a continuator of the great determinist. He has made a careful and critical estimate of Taine's work, and in view of its originality and the wide influence which it has exerted, he places its author upon a level with Comte, Spinoza, and Hegel.

LORENZO O'ROURKE.

Brooklyn, N Y.,
March, 10, 1906.

BALZAC

A CRITICAL STUDY

CHAPTER I

HIS LIFE AND CHARACTER

WORKS of genius are not merely the
offspring of the mind. The entire man
contributes to their production: his character, his education and his experience,
his past and present, his passions and
faculties, his virtues and vices, all the
phases of mind and action, leave their
trace in what he thinks and in what he
writes. To comprehend and judge Balzac
it is essential to have an acquaintance with
his life and his temperament, each of
which in turn has been the nurture of his
romances, and, like twin currents of sap,
has furnished the colors of that strange,
sickly and magnificent flower which I am
about to describe.

BALZAC—A CRITICAL STUDY

I

Balzac was a business man—and a business man involved in debt. From his twenty-first to his twenty-fifth year he had lived in a garret, occupied in writing tragedies and novels, of which he himself had but a poor opinion, opposed by his family, receiving from them very little money, earning less, threatened constantly with being condemned to a mechanical occupation, a declared incapable, and devoured by a longing for greatness and the consciousness of genius.[1] To be independent he turned speculator—first publisher, then printer, then type-founder. Everything fell short of success, and he saw final failure approaching. After four years of anguish, he wound up his business and began to write novels, to discharge the debts which were weighing him down. It was a horrible load which

---

[1] "Balzac d'après sa correspondance," by Mme. Surville, his sister.

he was forced to drag after him all his life. From 1827 to 1836 he was enabled to hold out by means of bills which, with great difficulty, he had renewed by the usurers. These latter he was compelled to divert, conciliate, overreach, and cajole. The unfortunate great man was often forced to play the comedy of "Mercadet" before he wrote it. All was of no avail. The debt, increased by interest, ever piled up. Toward the last his life, overwhelmed with fear, was endangered. In 1848 he said to Champfleury, who found him in an elegant mansion: "Nothing of all this belongs to me; these are friends who lodge me; I am their porter." Ever besieged and tormented, he performed prodigies of labor. He rose at midnight, drank some coffee, and worked a dozen hours in succession at one sketch,[1] after which he ran to the publishers and cor-

---

[1] He generally shut himself up for six weeks or two months, with shutters and curtains drawn, refusing to read his letters, and working sometimes eighteen hours

rected his proofs, dreaming the while of new schemes. He established two reviews, and practically edited one of them himself. Three or four times he essayed the drama. He evolved twenty speculative projects, and on one occasion rushed to Sardinia to satisfy himself whether or not the scoria of certains mines, exploited by the Romans, contained silver. Another time he thought that he had discovered a substance adapted for the manufacture of a new kind of paper, and made experiments with it. How would he pay his debts? How would he become rich? Wearied with bustle and misery, he would conjure in imagination some generous banker, a friend to letters, who would say to him: "Draw on my purse; pay your debts; be free. I have faith in your talent; I want to save a great man." He would then arrive at a state of exaltation, ended

a day by the light of four candles, wearing the white robe of a Dominican. ("Balzac," by Werdet, his publisher, p. 275.)

by believing in his dream, and saw himself
the greatest man in the world, member of
the Academy, deputy, minister. A moment
afterward, having redescended to earth,
he would rush to his writing table or to
his proofreading and plunge into his work
like a giant of toil. Sometimes, in the
midst of a conversation, he would suddenly
pause and upbraid himself. "Monster
without shame, you should be making copy
instead of talking!" Then he would reckon
up the money he had lost during these
wasted hours; so many lines at so much
a line, so much from the newspaper, so
much from the bookseller, so much for
the printing, so much for the re-printing;
the multiplied sum became enormous.

Money, everywhere money, forever
money; it was the persecutor and tyrant
of his life; he was its prey and slave,
whether by reason of necessity or honor
or imagination or hope. This master and
torturer bent him to his work, chained
him there, and even inspired him, pursued

him in his leisure, in his reflections, in his dreams,—directed his eyes, armed his hand, forged his poetry, animated his characters, and flooded all his work with its splendors. Thus obsessed and taught, he comprehended that money is the great mainspring of modern life. He was accustomed to reckon up the fortunes of his characters, explained their origin, their employment, and multiplication; he balanced receipts and expenses, and brought into his romances the methods of the counting house. He described speculation, purchase, sales, contracts, business ventures, inventions of industry, the combinations of stock-jobbing. He dissected lawyers, bailiffs, bankers; he brought in on all occasions the civil code and the bill of exchange. He made business romantic. He was the creator of combats equal to those of the heroes of antiquity, with this difference—that the prize was an inheritance, the soldiers were lawyers, and the code was the arsenal. Under his pen millions accumulated. Under his manipulation you saw fortunes swell, and swallow up their neighbors, exhibit themselves in gross parade, then overflow in luxury and power. The reader feels as tho he were gliding over cloth of gold. Hence a phase of his great success. He pictures the life that we are living, he speaks to us of the interests that concern us, he satiates the covetousness that possesses us.

II

HE was a Parisian in manners, mind, and inclination: this is the second trait. In this black ant-hill life is very active. Established democracy and a centralized government have drawn thither all the ambitions, and inflamed all ambitions. Money, glory, pleasure, heaped up and ready at hand, are the quarry for a multitude of insatiable desires which have been sharpened by expectation and rivalry.

Success! This word, unknown a century
ago, is to-day the sovereign master of all
lives. Paris is an arena into which one is
drawn involuntarily, as into a circus or
school; all else disappears at the thought
of rivals and the goal: the runner feels
upon his shoulders the breath of him behind; all his powers are strained; in this
access of will he doubles his effort and contracts the fever which both exhausts and
sustains him. Hence, prodigies of labor;
and not only the labor of the savant who almost breaks down in the pursuit of knowledge, or of the artist led into stupidity by
excess of invention, but the labor of the
man of special attainments who beguiles,
intrigues, calculates his words, measures
his friendships, and cunningly weaves the
thousand threads of his hopes into a net
for the purpose of obtaining a clientèle, a
place, or a name. We are indeed far removed from the time of our fathers, and
from those drawing-rooms where a pret-
tily-written letter, a clever madrigal, a

witty remark, made a whole evening interesting, or was the source of a fortune.
This is nothing; the fever of the brain is
still worse than the fever of the will. Since
the advent of the bourgeoisie all the professions have received the right of citizen-
ship; together with specialists, special
ideas have made their entrance into the
world; the current of thought is no longer
a petty stream of worldly slander, gallantry and amusing philosophy; it is a
large river which the bank, the business
house, chicanery, learning, have swollen
with their muddy waters; such is the tor-
rent which, pouring every morning into
each brain, both nourishes and drowns it.
Multiply all this by remembering that the
profound development of the sciences has
contributed millions of new facts, that increase of learning has enriched it with the
literatures and philosophies of other peoples, that all the ideas of the world here
converge as into a universal receptacle,—
and judge of its strength from the fact that

what has fed it are talents tried in the struggle and approved by success,—the wisest, the most powerful, the best furnished with inventive ability, the ablest thinkers. Whoever thinks is here. Academies, libraries, journals, the society of men of genius, the privilege of living unknown, draw hither all free and original spirits. On a bench in the Luxembourg you will hear a discussion on medicine. At the corner of yonder foot-path a geologist tells you the results of the latest excavations.

That museum indeed enables you to traverse all history in half an hour. An opera transports you among ideas which have been extinct for half a century. In two hours in a drawing-room you may pass in review all the opinions of humanity; here are mystics, atheists, communists, absolutists, all the extremes, all intermediaries, all shades. You will find no idea, whether strange, grand, or shallow, that has not engrossed the attention of

94

some man, fructified in his brain, and been
fortified with all the strength of folly or
reason. Specialties swarm, and with them,
monomanias. From all these brains which
seethe, thought issues like steam; involuntarily one breathes its atmosphere; it
sparkles in all these eyes, whether fixed or
restless, upon these faces, faded or wrinkled, in these gestures, nervous or studied;
those who arrive here for the first time
become dizzy; these streets are too elo-
quent; this crowd presses on too fast;
there are too many ideas revealed in the
windows, heaped up for sale, sculptured
in the monuments, staring from placards,
lighting up human faces—all of which
are encumbered and overloaded with
them; they issue from the bosom of waters calm and cool; they fall into a caldron
whence issues hissing steam, and where
rages a tempest of waves dashing against
one another and confined by quivering
walls of glowing metal. For this fever
of will and idea where is repose to be

found? In another fever, that of the senses.

In the country a man, weary from toil, goes to bed at nine o'clock; or, perhaps, he will sit by the fireside with his wife, or take a walk on the broad highway, peacefully and leisurely, wondering whether to-morrow will be fine. Think of Paris at this hour: the gas is lighted, the streets begin to fill, the theaters become jammed, the crowd is bent on enjoyment; wherever mouth or ears or eyes suspect pleasure it rushes; the pleasure, moreover, is studied and artificial, a sort of unhealthy food intended to excite, not to nourish, prepared by calculation and debauchery for the satiated and the corrupt. Even with regard to mental enjoyment all is too keen and excessive; the blasé taste must be awakened; there are needed paradoxical style, extravagant expressions, immodest suggestions, crude stories; anything else falls flat; reason must adopt the guise of a fool; the unexpected, the bizarre, the tormented and the exaggerated idea are the ordinary wear. All the secret wounds of the human soul and of history are probed; from the four corners of the world, from all the depths of life, from the heights of philosophy and art, are brought images, ideas, truth, paradox; all this mixture is brewed and the strange liquor which is distilled from it fills the veins with an unnatural, poisonous pleasure.

Balzac, while speaking of Paris, calls it "that great smoky ulcer exposed on both banks of the Seine." What man has breathed more of its exhalations than he? Who has struggled, thought and enjoyed more? What mind or heart has burned more with all those fevers? Especially that of desire. We have seen the horrible toil under which he lay chained, nights of labor numbered by the hundred, those unheard of expenses incurred by his inventions and scientific experiments, struggles with creditors, business persecutions, boundless yearning for greatness, universal ambition, exaltations, defeats, and the gulfs of despair in which he wallowed. What shall I say of his debauches of thought, of all those sciences that he dipped into, of all the trades he studied, of the philosophy that he invented, of the art that he sounded to its depths? Paris excites us too much, ordinary mortals as we are; what legions of ideas, then, must have crowded this brain which, fortified by inspiration and science, perceived in a gesture or garment a character and a whole life, placed them in their proper century, foresaw their future, read their character of painter, physician, philosopher, and spread the infinite network of his involuntary divinations over all ideas and facts!

Is it necessary to add that he had a special artistic sense that the romanticist invents for pleasure as for other things, —that he was a gourmand and glutton in luxury and enjoyment? Let one's private life, even after his death, remain veiled; nevertheless his taste for costly furniture will serve as an index.[1] He was a collector almost to the point of monomania; he had need of splendid books, antique furniture, carved tables, choice pictures; the gallery that he describes in "Cousin Pons" with a loving detail, was, they say, his own. He often condemned himself to cruel embarrassment for the sake of owning Saxony porcelains, tapestries, and other baubles. At the crisis of his first misfortune he wrote to his sister, "Ah, Laura! if you only knew how I dote (but keep it mum) on two blue screens embroidered with black (always mum)!" Tho tormented and worn out, he did not forget the screens: it was a fixed idea; "Always my screens!" His passion for beautiful

---

[1] See the description of his two apartments in M. Werdet's books. When he was at work in his white Dominican habit, he wore red morocco slippers bordered with gold; his body was encircled by a long Venitian gold chain, from which was suspended a gold folding stick, a gold knife, and a gold scissors.

things resembles a kind of physical itch-
ing; it is a sensual concupiscence rather
than a noble intellectual taste.

Such are his surroundings and his life;
you will divine what plants must sprout
from this soil so highly artificial and sea-
soned with such acrid flavors. Nothing
less was needed for the growth of that
enormous forest, for the empurpling of
those flowers of somber and metallic lus-
ter, for giving the fruits that strong and
biting taste. Many people suffer while
reading him. The style is painful, overcharged; ideas encumber and stifle one
another; complicated intrigues seize the
mind like an iron pincers; accumulated
passions roar and flame up like a furnace.
Out of this dim light there emerge and
stand out in violent relief a multitude of
grinning, twisted figures, more expressive,
more powerful, more animated than real
beings; among them a sordid vermin of
human insects, crawling lice, hideous bee-
tles, poisonous spiders born in corruption,

—digging, tearing, heaping up, devouring; hovering over all, there is revealed a dazzling fairyland and a melancholy nightmare created out of the material of the gigantic dreams that gold, science, art, glory, and power have conjured.

III

He died at the age of fifty, from apoplexy, caused by night-toil and the abuse of coffee, to which his forced watches condemned him. In order to publish within the space of twenty years ninety-seven works wrought out to so absolute a standard of perfection that he was accustomed to correct ten or twelve proofs ten or twelve times, he must have had a constitution as powerful as his intellect. His portraits show a thickset, robust man, with broad shoulders, abundant hair, a boldness of bearing, a sensual mouth; "his laugh was frequent and resounding, his teeth solid as iron." "He had the air," says Champfleury, "of a joyous wild boar." Animal life overflowed in him. We have seen too much of him in his novels. He risks there the minutest details of his secret history, not with the *sang froid* of the physiologist, but with the beaming eyes of the glutton or gourmand, who stands at the half-open door and devours with his eyes some fat and dainty morsel. The liberty afforded by the very ample contemporary Parisian style does not suffice for him.

He adopted that of Rabelais and Brantôme, so as to paint with the precision of the sixteenth century the coarseness of the sixteenth century, and composed his "Contes Drôlatiques," which are more than merely clever, and in which all the physical desires, unleashed and sated, defile before us like an illuminated bacchanal of Priapus. George Sand, having read the work, found it indecent. He called George Sand a prude, in good faith,—thus resembling La Fontaine, who could see nothing evil in his broad jests, and could never understand the reproaches of his confessor. It was, in fact, their native air; neither could he conceive how strangers found themselves ill-at-ease in that atmosphere. When a bird falls into the water, the fish are probably astonished that it can not breathe there. You see that this strength at times approaches grossness. His gayety, somewhat physical, is like that of a commercial traveler.

The day he conceived the idea of fusing all his novels into one to compose the "Human Comedy," he rushed to his sisters in the Rue Poissonière, all aglow with pleasure. "He entered, gesticulating like a drum-major with his great cornelian-headed cane, on which he had had engraved in Turkish this device of a sultan: *I am the conqueror of difficulties (briseur d'obstacles)*, and after imitating the booming of martial music and the rolling of a drum, he cried to us joyfully, 'congratulate me, for I am in a fair way to become a genius.' "

His letters, so affectionate, have something of the trivial. His pleasantries are heavy.[1] He gesticulates, hums a tune, taps people on the stomach, plays the buffoon. His verve is that of an operator. He only had to exaggerate its traits to furnish that of Bixiou and Vautrin. All this came of a nature too full, a sap too exuberant, which overflowed in movements, enjoyments, inventions, labors, not too delicate,

---

[1] "I have good news to tell you, little sister; the reviews are paying me better for my articles. He! he! —Werdet tells me that my 'Country Doctor' was sold out in eight days. Ha! ha!—I have wherewith to make faces at the November and December bills that disturb you. Ho! ho!—Ah! there are many millions in 'Eugénie Grandet!' But since the story is true, you do not want me to improve on the truth, do you? I am going to try the drama; I shall begin with 'Marie Touchet,' a bold theme which I shall supply with local characters. Halt, there, Death! If you come, let it be to help me bear my burden; I have not yet finished my task."—WERDET.

at times even brutal,[1] and always impossible to control. He told to all who came in his way his literary projects, his plans even in detail, and what was worse, his business projects, for example, his idea of exploiting the ancient mines of Sardinia; naturally, this last was stolen from him. He admired himself naïvely and in public: "You bear a likeness to me," said he to Champfleury. "I am glad of this resemblance for your sake." He then added, "There are only three men in Paris who know their language: Hugo, Gautier and I."

At fourteen years of age he had already announced his future celebrity. When in letters or conversation he speaks of his novels, the word *masterpiece* recurs

---

[1] One day at dinner a young writer having said to him: "We men of letters," Balzac exploded in a formidable burst of laughter and roared at him: "You, sir, you, a man of letters! What a claim to make! What foolish presumption! You, you compare with us! Come, come! Do you forget, sir, with whom you have the honor of sitting? With the marshals of modern literature."—WERDET.

naturally and continually,—perches on his pen or upon his lips. He regards himself as universal; had he not, in "Louis Lambert," uttered the last word in philosophy and science? He dreams of a place in the Institute, the Chamber of Peers, the Ministry. "Are not those who have made the tour of the world of ideas the most fitted to govern men? I would like to see the man who would be astonished if I should receive a portfolio."

This boasting,[1] which stands out in enormous characters in all his prefaces, is only awkward; every one has his own phase of it, with this difference, that by prudence and good taste each one conceals it and slips quietly and politely through this crowded drawing room we call the world; Balzac, being a great strong man, pushes roughly ahead, trampling on peo-

---

[1]He had a statue of Napoleon in his room, and on the scabbard of the sword were these words: "What he could not accomplish by the sword, I will accomplish by the pen." Signed: Honoré de Balzac.—WERDET.

ple's feet, and hustling the crowd. It is not insolence, but mere carelessness. When there is cause he permits himself to be contradicted, he endures blame, he thanks sincere counsellors. He laughs himself at his vauntings, and after a little reflection tolerates them; the only hateful pride is the pride of a tyrant; and he was good, a child even, and therefore a good child, removed as far as possible from pride and hardness, a schoolboy in his relaxations, an idler on occasion, naïf, capable of playing trivial games and of enjoying them with all his heart. His family letters are truly touching; there can be no more beautiful or natural example of affection than his attachment for his sister. Its natural outpouring is complete and profound.[1]

Sensuality, rudeness, triviality, jovial

[1] "Tell my mother I love her as much as when I was a child; tears come into my eyes as I write these lines, tears of tenderness and despair, for I foresee the future, and this devoted mother is necessary to me in the day of triumph. Take good care of our mother, Laura, both now and in the future."

gayety, boasting, goodness—all these are
different results of his expansive nature;
there remains one which enlists in its service all the others—his passion for invention, his enthusiastic and inexhaustible
imagination. His head was a volcano of
projects, visions that he fell in love with
and then deserted for still more beautiful
ones, dreams of wealth and glory, business
combinations, reforms in politics, language and science, systems of administration, adventures, errors and truths on all
subjects, startling and splendidly embroidered pyrotechnics that revealed and lighted
up a whole century and a world. His life,
his character, and his surroundings point-
ed his way to the realm of romance of
which he took possession as of a kingdom,
by right of nature and by right of will.

CHAPTER II

THE GENIUS OF BALZAC

WHEN we speak of a man's genius *(esprit)* we mean the general shaping of his thought. There is in every one a certain ruling habit which obliges him to look here or there, which suggests to him a figure of speech, a philosophical reflection, or a jest—so that no matter what he may be working at, he falls into one of these habits by the very necessity of his nature, his mind and his taste. Savants call this method; artists call it talent. Let us examine it in Balzac.

I

He began in the fashion not of artists, but of savants. Instead of painting, he dissected. He did not enter into the souls of his characters violently and at a single bound like Shakespeare or Saint-Simon; he walked round and round them patiently and slowly like an anatomist, lifting a muscle, then a bone, then a nerve, and only reaching the brain and heart after he had traversed the whole cycle of the organs and their functions. He described the city, then the street, then the house. He described the foundations, the front, the structure and the materials of the entrance, the jutting of the plinths, the color of the moss, the rust on the bars, the cracks in the windows. He notes the arrangement of the rooms, the shape of the chimneys, the age of the tapestries, the quality and arrangement of the furniture; then he would expatiate on the clothes. Arrived at his character, he exhibited the structure of his hands, the curve of his spine, the shape of his nose, the size of his bones, the length of his chin, the size of his lips. He counted his gestures, his winks, his warts. He knew his origins, his education, his history; how much he had

in land and income, what circle he moves
in; what people he saw, what he spends,
what he ate, the brands of his wines, who
formed his kitchen force,—in brief, the innumerable multitude of circumstances infinitely ramified and intersected, which go
to make up, influence, and modify the sur-
face and the depths of nature and human
life. There was in him an archæologist,
an architect, an upholsterer, a tailor, a cos-
tumer, an auctioneer, a physiologist, and
a notary: all these make their appearance
in turn, each one reading his report, the
most detailed in the world and the most
exact. The artist listened with pains and
scrupulous care, and his imagination did
not take fire until he had made out of this
infinite paper scaffolding a solid structure
according to his idea and desire. "I am,"
said he, "a doctor of the social sciences."
A pupil of Geoffroy Saint-Hilaire, he announced[1] his project of writing a natural
history of man. Animals have been cata-

[1]Preface of "The Human Comedy."

logued, he would furnish the inventory
of manners. He has done it; the history
of art has never presented an idea so foreign to art, nor a work of art so great;
he has almost equaled the immensity of
his subject by the immensity of his erudition.

Hence numerous defects and merits;
in many passages he bores many readers.
I said, a moment ago, that there is a
crowd of artisans and bailiffs in his waiting room; we are there with them and it
is disagreeable to be kept waiting in an
anteroom. The artist keeps us too long;
you feel like swearing at him when he
keeps you waiting in the cold for an hour
among a crowd of his employés. This
crew, nevertheless, is nothing if not di-
verting. Memoirs of carpenters and stories of lawyers, however, end by giving
you a headache; the odor of the registry-
office, the courtroom and the shop becomes suffocating. One must be an observer by profession, a critic for instance,

or still better, a business man, to be at home in this atmosphere. If we were not all plebeians and amateurs of science we would have flung up M. Goriot at the beginning of his fatal apoplexy, and flung Cæsar Birotteau into the fire at the first deficit of his balance sheets; the author would have seen the half of his public vanish if the nineteenth century had not invested cataplasms and bills of protest with a sort of romance.

But the worst of it is that the book often becomes obscure. A description is not a painting, and Balzac often thinks that he has produced a picture, when he has merely given a description. His compilations reveal nothing; they are merely catalogs; the enumeration of the stamens of a flower, never brings before our eyes the image of the flower. It requires the poetical faculty of George Sand or Michelet, or the violent sorcery of Victor Hugo or Dickens, to conjure in our minds the shape of physical objects;

such writers transport us beyond ourselves, and emotion places all in a clear
light. The minute explanations of Balzac leave us in quiet and in darkness. It
is in vain that he describes so minutely; the
intersections of the bars of the Hôtel du
Guénic, or the nose of the Chevalier de
Valois; these crossbars and this nose remain obscure; only a physiologist or an
archaeologist might divine something; the
common run of readers will pause,
mouths open in respectful astonishment,
secretly wishing for the aid of some
sketch or portrait.

A final misfortune is that the description carried at too great length falsifies
the impression. When the imagination
perceives an imaginary character it is as
if by a flash of lightning; if you linger
over a trait or a feature, through a dozen
lines, nothing at all is perceived. One no
longer knows whether the figure is lovely, grandiose or fine. Its physiognomy
has disappeared; there remains a mere

bundle of flesh and bones. Is it a woman that you see here, or is it not rather a mass of anatomical shreds?

"The arch of the strongly penciled brows extended over both eyes, the flame of which scintillated momentarily like that of a fixed star; the white of the eye is not of a bluish tinge, nor sown with red veins, nor is it of a pure white; it has the *consistency of horn,* but is of a warm tone; the pupil of the eye is bordered with a circle of orange; it is like *bronze surrounded with gold*—but living gold, animated bronze. This pupil is deep; it is not double as in certain eyes, nor has it that metallic cast which reflects the light, resembling the eyes of tigers or cats. This depth has something of the infinite, just as *eyes reflected in a mirror* have a suggestion of the absolute." The portrait is continued thus through two hundred lines. A friend of mine, a naturalist, asked me one day to come and see a magnificent specimen butterfly that he had just been experimenting with. I found it cut into about thirty pieces, pinned separately to a paper. Those disgusting bits, when put together, formed the magnificent butterfly.

Nevertheless what power there is in all this! What striking qualities and what relief this interminable enumeration gives to the character! How we recognize him in every action and in every detail! How real he becomes! With what precision and energy he becomes imprinted in our memory! How thoroughly he resembles nature, and how perfect the illusion! For such is nature; its details are infinite and infinitely drawn out; the inner man leaves his imprint on his external life, on his house, on his furniture, on his business, his gestures, his language; it is necessary to explain this multitude of effects in order to wholly explain him. And on the other hand, it is necessary to bring together this multitude of causes in order to present him in his completeness. The food which nourishes you, the air which you breathe, the buildings that surround you, the books that you read, the most trivial habits in which you give a glimpse of yourself, the most imperceptible circumstances which you allow to influence you—all contribute to make you the man that you are; an infinite amount of endeavor has been concentrated in the formation of your character, and your character is revealed in an infinite number of endeavors; your soul is a crystal lens which gathers to a focus all the luminous rays darted from the boundless universe, and like a radiator, reflects them back into infinite space.

It is on this account that every man is a being apart, absolutely distinct, capable of being multiplied to an enormous extent, a sort of abyss whose depth is equaled only by his prophetic genius and enormous erudition. I dare to assert that in this respect Balzac has mounted to the level of Shakespeare. His characters live; they enter into familiar conversation; Nucingen, Rastignac, Philippe Bridau, Phellion, Bixiou, and a hundred others are men whom we have seen, whom we cite to give an idea of some real person, whom we meet in the street. As he himself says of original artists, he has created "emulation in civic life."

If he is so strong it is because he is systematic; this is a second trait which completes the savant; in him the philosopher is combined with the observer. Along with the details he sees the laws which connect them. His houses and his physiognomies are the molds in which he fashions the souls of his characters. In these all things are inter-related; there is always some passion or situation which is at the bottom of them, and which prescribes what happens. This is why they leave so powerful an impression; each action and detail concurs to drive it home; tho innumerable, they are brought together for a unique effect. We feel them all in a single sensation; the characters are more expressive than actual living beings. They concentrate what nature has dispersed. This is still more apparent in his plots. His order is admirable; it required an extraordinary power of comprehension to connect all these events, to maneuver this army of characters, to combine these long series of machinations and intrigues. He is like a circus driver who reins in fifty powerful and spirited horses, keeping them to their course, without lessening their speed. Many of his plots are so skilfully contrived that one loses his way in them; it is necessary to be a merchant to understand "Cæsar Birotteau," and one needs to be a magistrate to follow "Une Ténébreuse Affaire;" the latter is beyond the sounding of ordinary faculties, it is a concert so rich, composed of so many novel instruments and of so varied and intricate ideas, that our ears, accustomed to the simplicity of the classics, can with difficulty grasp the ensemble and conception of the composer.

Moreover, and what is still more notable, he always has some great idea which serves as the center round which his story revolves. He may be wrong in announcing it, but the announcement does not deceive. He not only describes, he thinks. It is not enough to observe life, he understands it. Celibacy, marriage, government, finance, luxury, ambition, all the leading occupations, all the secret depths of passion: such are the foundations of his work; he is the philosopher of humanity. Take "Père Goriot," for example; nothing could be more individual than its characters; nothing could be further removed from those vague beings and pure abstractions which metaphysical novelists deck out in the guise of mankind. But who does not see amid the life, details, and surroundings of the individual, the abridged history of the nineteenth century, the struggles of a young man, poor, ambitious, and capable, oscillating between obedience and revolt, seeing on one side a father, "the Christ of paternity," who lies dying on a sordid pallet, betrayed by his daughters and abandoned by all; on the other a grandiose brigand, "the Cromwell of the bagnios," equipped with all the allurements that genius, opportunity and experience can gather together? And who fails to recognize in this characteristic history of our century the eternal history of the soul, Shakespeare's Hamlet, the generous young man endowed with the family affections and the illusions of youth, who, fallen unexpectedly into the mire of life, chokes, struggles, weeps, and ends in resignation or suffocation.

But what truly stamps him philosopher and lifts him to the level of the greatest artists, is the unification of all his works into a unique whole. Each novel is connected with the others, the same characters reappear; the whole is bound together; we have a drama with a hundred scenes, each one recalling the others. Notice this from the title. On every page you grasp the whole human comedy. The landscape is such that it can be seen entire at every turn. The characters rise before your imagination, surrounded by the innumerable train of circumstances associated with them. You view at a glance their family relations, their nationality, the sources of their authority and of their means. Never has artist concentrated so much light upon the countenance he was painting. Never has artist so made up for the essential shortcomings of art. For the isolated drama or novel only gives a one-sided idea of history and explains nature badly. It merely scoops an event out of the vast conglomerate of things, suppressing all the shreds and ligatures that bind it to adjacent things. In selecting it mutilates, and in reducing the model it spoils it.

HIS GENIUS

To be exact, therefore, is to be great. Balzac has grasped the truth because he has grasped the whole. His great talent for system has given his pictures unity as well as power, faithfulness to life as well as interest. This talent involves many an absurdity. You are in the midst of a pretty scene; all at once there comes a shower of metaphysics. You dry yourself, grumbling, and hurriedly skip a few pages. One is following a fine train of thought; all of a sudden there supervenes one of those fantastic laws improvised by the imagination, and imposed in the name of science.[1] We have finished a piquant and touching comedy, a description of the life of a poor canon expelled from his provincial boarding-house; without the

---

[1] "Natalie had that roundness of form which, tho a sign of strength, is the infallible index of a will which often reaches infatuation in the case of persons of weak and narrow intellectual powers. Her hands, like those of a Greek statue, confirmed the presage of her face and physique, in announcing a spirit of illogical domination, willing for the sake of willing."

slightest warning we are plunged into such emphatic balderdash as this: "No doubt in another age Troubert would have been a Hildebrand or an Alexander VI. We are living in an age in which defective government has made man to fit society, instead of making society for man. There exists an eternal struggle between the individual and the system whose aim is to exploit him, and which he, in turn, endeavors to exploit for his own profit; so that in former times the man, really more free, showed more concern for the public welfare. The circle of human action has been insensibly enlarged; the mind capable of embracing its synthesis will always be a distinguished exception, for, in the moral as in the physical world, motion loses in intensity what it gains in extent. Society can not found itself upon exceptions. In the beginning man was purely and simply paternal, and his heart, beating warmly, was centered in the bosom of his family.

Later on he began to live for a clan or for a small commonwealth."

All this apropos of two canons, and a good man in despair because he can't find his slippers. When Balzac is philosophical he is obscure; when he is learned he is a pedant.

II

Such are the materials of the work. When the observer and philosopher has thus heaped up the ideas and facts, the artist arrives upon the scene. By degrees he warms up; the characters take on form and color; they begin to live. After reasoning comes feeling. Balzac involuntarily divines their gestures. Their sayings, their actions take form of themselves in his brain. Heat enters the heavy mass of metal which has been accumulated from such distances and at cost of so much anxiety. It melts and flows into the mold, and there appears a new and brilliant statue. But after what struggles, and at the cost of what labor! Balzac has none of the passion, the sudden and happy inspiration, the rich and facile divination of the true and the beautiful. By nature he is obscure; his expression is involved; his first jet is muddy, interrupted, uncertain; he boils like water enclosed in a vessel by a heavy cover which it stirs by fits and starts but can not lift. His heavy physical nature seems to oppress his native invention; he has struggled as much with himself as with external things. He wrote fifty volumes of bad romances, which he knew to be bad, before he entered upon his "Human Comedy." We have just seen the mass of studies, a sort of subterranean foundation which supports each of his works, and we remember that he corrected, filed, recast until he made them illegible, from ten to a dozen proofs of each novel.

Nevertheless all this care has not been

sufficient. His characters do not all live;
sometimes in those that are most alive a
false action or phrase indicates that inspiration has flagged; the fire in his furnace was not intense enough; dross has
persisted and many of his finest and most
muscular figures are marred and flawed.
He does not merge his own personality
in his characters instantly and spontaneously; this is only reached by degrees;
sometimes he pauses on the way and
beneath the garb of his character you
perceive Balzac himself. The "Memoirs
of Two Young Married Women," Farra-
besche in "The Village Curate," Father
Fourchon in "The Peasants," nearly all
his great men, nearly all his women,
whether honest or frail, are imperfectly
molded figures that should have been
recast. The Parisian man of the world,
the refined observer and encyclopedist,
the amateur physiologist of moral diseases, the hazy philosopher, the naturalist and the mystic, pierce through these

different masks. The tirades of Madame de Mortsauf are almost as disagreeable as the conceits of Shakespeare. The Countess Honorine, who dies from excess of modesty, writes, while dying, the most indecent of letters. Madame Claës, on her deathbed, lets fall physiological allusions and metaphysical axioms of which, happily, she was incapable. Poor Eugénie Grandet, provincial, naïve, almost cloistered, so reserved, so pious, so high minded, writes to her cousin who has forsaken her so suddenly and coarsely, these incredible words: "Be happy after the manner of the conventions of society to which you have sacrificed our early passion (*nos premières amours*)." Her ink would have dried up before she found the first half of this phrase. She would have dashed her inkstand to pieces rather than write the last three words.

Usually, however, he issues out of himself and becomes his character. His rage for work triumphs over all obstacles. The artist, held in restraint by the scholar, gets the upper hand. Torn from his bed at midnight, seated at his desk for twelve hours in succession, locked up in his house for two months at a time, losing consciousness of external objects so that he no longer recognizes the neighboring streets, he becomes drunk with his work[1] —his imagination is flooded with it; he is haunted by his characters, obsessed by them, sees them in visions; they live and move in him with such reality and intensity that henceforth they develop of themselves with the independence and necessity of real beings. Roused, he remains half submerged in his dream. He almost believes in the events which he relates: "I leave for Alençon, for Grenoble, where Mlle. Carmon and M. Bénassis live." He comes to tell his friends news of his imaginary world, just as one gives news of the real world: "Do you know

---

[1] "I have not a single idea, I do not take a step outside of Physiology. I dream of it; I do nothing else."

who Félix Vandenesse is to marry? A young lady named Grandville. It is an excellent marriage, that; the Grandvilles are wealthy in spite of what Mlle. de Bellefeuille has cost this family."

It was essential to have this power of illusion to create souls.[1] Imaginary beings are born, exist and act under the same conditions as real beings. They are born of the systematic agglomeration of an infinite number of ideas, as the others are born of the systematic agglomeration of an infinite number of causes. They act through the independent and unreflecting impulse of constituent ideas, as the others act by the personal and spontaneous force of generating causes. Thus

---

[1] One day Jules Sandeau, returning from a trip, alluded to his sister, who was ill. Balzac listened some time, then said to him: "All this is interesting, my friend, but *let us return to reality;* let us talk of Eugénie Grandet." On another occasion, Balzac, at the home of Mme. Sophie Gay, was describing a superb black horse that he would like to present to Sandeau. He wound up by believing that he had given it to Sandeau, and, later, asked Sandeau for news of it, etc.—WERDET.

the character actually detaches himself
from the author, influences him, leads
him, and the intensity of the hallucination
is the unique source of truth.

I believe that this species of genius is
the greatest of all. There is no other
that assembles more things in less space.
One act, one word of Vautrin, Bixiou,
Grandet, Hulot, Mme. Marneffe, implies
and recalls all their natural traits and all
the circumstances of their lives. You
will then perceive, as in a lightning flash,
vast and most unexpected truths, the psychology of temperaments, of sex, of passion, the whole man and humanity along
with man: they are foreshortened
abysses. I shall cite, later, many examples of all this; here are two only. I refer
to that philosopher of the bagnio, a sort
of Iago, tho less wicked and more dangerous, who has raised perversity to the
plane of philosophy, and preaches it with
all the enthusiasm of genius and depravity. He is laying before Rastignac the

budget of an intriguer of the fashionable world: "Your laundry will cost you a thousand francs; *love and religion require fine linen on their altars.*" Shortly after, having almost succeeded in seducing him to commit murder, he offers to shake hands. "Rastignac quickly drew back his own, and, turning pale, sank upon a chair. He seemed to see a pool of blood before him. *'Ah! we have still a few streaks of virtue left,'* said Vautrin in a low voice. 'Papa d'Oliban has three millions, I know his fortune. The dowry will make you as white as a wedding garment, even in your own eyes.'" I do not believe that cynicism and misanthropy ever invented words more poignant.

Here is another example: Balthazar Claës, a rich Fleming, becomes a chemist, almost an alchemist, an atheist; one day his wife forces her way into his laboratory, in the midst of a dangerous experiment; he throws himself upon her, lifts her like a feather, gains the staircase amid the reports of shattered glass, and sits on the steps, exhausted. "My dear," says he, "I had forbidden you to come here? *The saints have preserved you from death.*"

You see in this state of prostration the artificial man has disappeared; childish superstitions alone persist; he talks as if he were twelve years old.

There are, as a matter of fact, many examples of cerebral derangement in which the knowledge of acquired languages is suppressed, and only the mother tongue persists; the superstructure of ideas has crumbled, leaving only the old foundations. Apparently, Balzac did not dream here of this detail of pathology; but inspiration is a kind of divination.

You have seen at times an ugly caterpillar with numberless claws and tireless teeth, lying asleep and undergoing transformation in the thick cocoon which envelops it; it issues forth painfully a heavy butterfly, weighed by the débris of its

133

chrysalis, tho borne into the upper air on its magnificent and enormous wings. Such is Balzac, sustained and dulled by the gross vigor of his temperament, and the accumulated stores of his knowledge, and whose genius only unfetters itself by dint of patience after a thousand reverses, with visible imperfections, by the multiplied triumphs of his will.

CHAPTER III

I

When you bring Balzac to the attention of a man of taste, who knows French well and has been nourished on the classics, you have before you a little comedy like this:

Our man handles with some dread these sixteen huge volumes. Here are many things to read, and things that are new; the moderns write too much. Has not La Bruyère already complained that everything has been said? What has this newcomer been able to discover that he should tell it at such length?

Nevertheless he ventures cautiously, and, by way of experiment, turns a few chance pages; he happens on this passage: "The most exquisite materialism is stamped on all the Flemish customs."

He opens his eyes wide at this, having never seen the stamp of this stern thing, materialism; he reflects for a moment, and translates the passage for himself in a low voice; this must doubtless mean: "The Flemings are refined in their customs of life."

Somewhat startled, he opens another volume and reads: "It is impossible to avoid the material and social dilemma which results from this balance sheet of public virtue with regard to marriage." This is uncouth. Doubtless, M. de Balzac would have done better to say simply: "Married women are not all virtuous; this is an evil, but it is a good as well, for without it men would bow too low."

For the sake of a diversion (these translations are painful), he asks for a simple little piece of description; he is told to turn over to the "Curé of Tours," where there is a devout and mischief-making old maid; probably M. de Balzac will speak of her entertainingly. He encounters this introduction: "No creature of the feminine gender was better equipped than Mademoiselle Sophie Gamard to represent the elegiac nature of the old maid."

"Creature," "feminine gender," "elegiac nature!" he exclaims. "Am I in an anthropological museum?" He turns the page and his eyes rest on this pretty passage: "Such was the substance of the words poured out in advance from the *capillary tubes* of the grand female consistory."

"Decidedly, this is a course in botany; what sort of a hornet's nest have I been led into?"

He skips twenty pages, and with increasing astonishment reads the last page thrice: "That apparent egotism of men who are the bearers of a new science, a nation or a code of laws—is it not the noblest of passions, and in some sort the maternity of the masses? For in order to give birth to a new people, or to produce a new world of ideas, is it not essential that they should unite in their powerful heads the breasts of woman and the power of God?"

He has never conceived of men with breasts in the head. He beats his own in confusion; his arms fall to his sides, and he regards with a smile of pity his unfortunate friend who thinks that fine.

He takes breath, and at the end of a half hour again takes up the task. He meets with "ineradicable convictions," the "throbbing pangs of a cancer" which gnaws the soul, "a labial telegraph." He finds that the traveling salesman is "a species of human dynamite, an unbelieving priest, who on that account but speaks the better of his mysteries and his dogmas." He learns during the sale of two hats, "that a nation with two chambers, that a woman who listens with both ears, are equally lost, that Eve and the serpent are an eternal symbol of a daily fact which began and shall probably end with the world." He concludes that the history of a traveling salesman gives occasion for much fine moralizing, and accepts it as a fact that M. de Balzac is a pedantic encylclopedist; if you tolerate his big words, his scientific jargon, his philosophic rhapsody, it is for the same reason that you endure rain in November. There remain two things to endure.

He opens "Eugénie Grandet." Every one has told him that this is a masterpiece in the simple style. Assuredly the introductory passage will be simple; introductions always are; let us look at this: "There are to be found in certain provinces houses whose aspect inspires a kind of melancholy equal to that roused by the gloomiest cloisters, the dreariest landscapes, or the saddest ruins. Perhaps, in reality, these houses contain the silence of the cloister, the austerity of such landscapes, and the dead bones of such ruins."

What a beginning! M. de Balzac lifts up his voice and announces the show with the heavy and formidable solemnity of some mountebank.

Our poor reader keeps his patience; with an air of resignation he begins another novel almost as celebrated, "The Lily in the Valley," one of the author's favorites: "To what genius, nourished by tears, shall we be indebted for that tenderest of elegies, the story of torments endured in silence by souls whose tender roots came in contact with the flinty soil of the domestic hearth, whose first blossomings are torn away by cruel hands, whose flowers are killed by the frost at the moment of their opening!"

What a number of figures occur in the first few lines; these metaphors are stirring very early in the day! M. de Balzac is like a painter who empties a pot of red pigment over his canvas before he begins to paint. The reader gets a headache and decides that this style is laid on too thick, that it indicates a laborious and ungraceful writer, one who is a colorist to order and in spite of himself. In this relation consider these passages chosen from twenty similar ones: "All the manufactories of intellectual products have discovered a certain spice, a special kind of ginger, which is their delight. Hence prizes and hoped-for dividends; hence those stolen ideas which, like the slave merchants of Asia, the caterers to the public taste, snatch half-hatched from the engendering brain, and drag in a disheveled state before their worn-out sultan, their *Shahabaham,* that terrible public, which, if it is not amused cuts off their head in withholding their bag of gold." M. de Balzac would be a poet; he is so eager that his eagerness overreaches him; he trenches on enigma. "Caroline is a second edition of Nabuchadonosor; for one day, like the royal chrysalis, she will pass from the cocoon of the beast to the imperial purple." This means that a foolish woman may become wicked. The daughters of Gorgibus spoke thus.

More effort; how much it costs to begin a study of great modern authors! Formerly one entrusted himself safely to the pages of a good book; nowadays, the gate is obstructed by abstractions and metaphors about as ornamental and convenient as a swamp of brushwood.

This is how "A Bachelor's Establishment" begins: "In 1790 the middle class of Issoudoun rejoiced in a physician named Rouget, who passed for a man of deep wickedness." *Rejoiced!* Only porters still say "You rejoice in poor health." Not being a porter, I do not care to be addressed in this style.

Our reader, taking heart of grace, continues, and turning the pages here and there, finds phrases like this (the story concerns an old colonel, who in doing a kindness, breaks his pipe): "The angels might have gathered up the fragments of the pipe." Or this: "She permitted herself that smile of resigned women which pierces granite." The words *sublime, dazzling superhuman,* recur on every page. Decidedly M. de Balzac has bad manners; he is coarse and a charlatan; he has the loud laugh and strident voice of the plebeian; his style shocks or stuns; in order to be strenuous he forces it; you see him warming up to his work; all this is unwholesome, and I give up the task.

Thereupon he returns you the sixteen volumes and says: "When I read an author it is as if I admit into my home a well-bred man understanding the art of conversation. M. de Balzac talks like a dictionary of arts and crafts, like a manual of German philosophy, and an encyclopedia of natural sciences. If, perchance, he forgets this jargon, he relapses into a rough workman who indulges in horseplay and bluster. If at last the artist emerges, I have before me a man of enthusiastic, violent, unhealthy temperament, whose ideas burst forth in painful explosions, and whose style is overcharged, tortured and extravagant. Not one of these persons know how to talk, and I admit none of them to my salon."

This judgment, thoroughly French and classic, derives its habits of life and thought from the seventeenth century; it is based on two suppositions: that an author speaks to men of the world and that these men form their ideas by analysis.

In effect examine, in turn, the habits of the school of analysis and of society. In a drawing-room the first obligation is not to displease; the second, to please. All technical terms must be avoided among gentlemen, and especially among ladies, for the reason that they will not be understood; technical terms used in chemistry, zoölogy, or finance, have the same effect in a parlor as siphons, skeletons, or bankbooks displayed on the flower-stands and sofas; self-respect would not permit

you to understand them; good taste
would be shocked at these incongruities;
delicacy would shrink from these remind-
ers of toil and money. You must, then,
avoid all the jargon of metaphysics; you
would have the air of a professor; an
evening party is not a school; besides,
people are there to enjoy themselves, and
philosophy was never yet amusing; you
must above all avoid rough gestures and
loud speech. The people who come here
are rich, or at least of the leisure class,
and cultured; they form a sort of aristocracy; and an aristocracy, by reason of
its pride, reserve, and delicate tastes, re-
jects with horror all that smells of the
shop. In fine, you must be polite, and the
man of politeness avoids the airs of a
great man, the pretentious tone, the af-
fected and imperious attitudes which at-
tract notice and demand respect.

Moreover, when men form their ideas
by analysis, they only think step by step;
a leap trips them; they require and make

use of transitions always. They do not at all relish being thrown from a bank into an astronomical problem, or falling, without warning, from a palace into a shop. They demand that an idea shall follow naturally the one that precedes it, that each page shall reveal ideas of the same species and the same order, that in order to arrive at general truths the author shall ascend the ladder of all subordinated and secondary truths, that he shall first describe familiar and daily events, and that by degrees and unconsciously, he shall suggest to the reader elevated and novel reflections. He would limit him to the comparison of noble things with noble things only, of the vile with the vile; religious subjects should inspire serious figures, and jovial ones joyful images. They would choose words according to their root and usage, make use of the simplest only, imitate on all occasions the Latin and antique style, strive unceasingly for exactness and clearness. They have a horror of exaggerated comparisons, violent expressions, the coupling of incongruous words, paradoxes of style, strange phrases, refinements, facts of the imagination. They would be spoken to in a sort of elegant algebra, they would have an even flow of successive ideas, one blending with the other, so that the meaning would appear without effort, without straining and without mishap.

Certainly Balzac is bound to displease persons who hold such ideas and follow this ideal of life. But it may be answered that all men do not hold these opinions nor lead this kind of life. Change the environment of habits and ideas: on the instant, all the laws of style are changed. In place of a drawing-room, imagine a political club; angry warfare, bitter sarcasms, profound and hateful passions, the coarseness and vulgarity of practical minds, will usurp the place of elegance and refinement. Now, instead of talkers

who merely criticise, place there painters
who have imagination. Instantly, sudden
and atrocious outbursts of wit, raw, glittering or trivial metaphors take the place
of measured and regular development.
Further, if you import into the club the
language of the drawing-room you will
appear overrefined and insipid; you will
be called a coxcomb or a dancing-master.
If you talk to painters in the manner of
the critic, you will seem tiresome and
dreary; you will be called an academician
and a prater. Good style is the art of
making one's self listened to and understood; this art varies with the auditory;
the very thing that displeases one pleases
another; what is obscure and tiresome
for one is clear and full of charm for another. No one has the right to impose
his pleasures and his tastes upon another;
no one has the right to copy his pleasures
and his tastes from another. There is,
then, an infinite number of good styles.
There are as many as there are epochs,

nations and great minds. All differ. If you were to write to-day in the manner of Herodotus or Homer, you would be treated as childish; if you were to speak to-day in the fashion of Isaias or Job, people would fly from you as from a madman. The barriers that separate ages and ideas are as strong as those that divide species and instincts. The diversity of nature is as responsible for the diversity of instincts in the one as it is for the diversity of literary style in the other; social history is but a prolongation of natural history. The pretension to judge all styles by a single standard is as preposterous as the proposition to shape all minds in a single mold and to reconstruct all ages after a single plan.

Consider, therefore, the auditory of Balzac and the structure of his mind. You would impose upon him the manners of the drawing-room; but are there drawing-rooms to-day? I see that there is still a grand salon with flowers, a piano, wax

candles; but that is all. After dinner the
men go off to smoke; or if they remain,
you will find them gathered in a corner,
or in little groups. They talk politics,
railroads, a little literature, much business. They have come "in order to keep
up to date and to exchange views on
things." From time to time some one
leaves the group and goes over to talk to
the ladies, who form a lonely circle round
the fire. The abolishment of gallantry
and of the court has brought them to this
pass; they no longer talk of anything except dress and music. At a reception
how many men dance after they have
reached the age of twenty-five? And
in truth they are in the right. There are
lacking the red cheeks of the Chevalier de
Grammont, his cloak of flaming red or emerald, his lace, his ribbons, and his gilt;
their funereal black clothes, their look of
care, their smile to order, are repugnant to
the custom; in fine, they are not at ease
except among themselves; their real salon

is a club, where, wearied with business accounts, science, or toil, they can retire and read the newspapers. Specialists mostly, they rub against specialists of every description, and the trade jargon is not offensive to them. All philosophies and literatures distilled in periodicals, conversation, and the thousand means of publicity which nourish life in Paris, flow over them. Paris is at once the reservoir and the alembic in which are engulfed and refined the ideas of the whole world. Thus fed and sated, they can find pleasure in every order of ideas, and they are not satisfied with ideas unless these are expressed in striking forms. They wish to be distracted and moved; they have need of novelty, singularity, and surprising situations. I acknowledge, however, that there remains to them a stock of moderation, refinement, and elegance. Balzac, I admit, by his strangeness of expression, his pedantry, his obscurity, his exaggeration, often goes beyond what their taste demands. No matter; here is a public, original, complete, distinct from others, and having the rights of others. If it has its defects, it has also its merits. If it is less polished and amiable than that of old, it is more learned, it has a more open mind, it is more skilled in literature. You see clearly that Balzac has the right to be violent and bizarre, an encyclopedist and a philosopher, that his habits of style correspond to our habits of life, and that the writer is authorized by the public.·

Consider, now, the writer. You would fain impose upon him your methods of analysis. But he has his own, since he is an artist, and his are as good as yours, since, like you, he makes himself understood by his equals. Your mind resembles the table of contents of a good book on zoölogy or physics; the ideas fall into order of themselves in a continuous, progressive series. They take form, divided off and classified; they take their departure forthwith and naturally. Each has its compartment prepared beforehand, and each family enters its place without losing one of its own members, and unaccompanied by any stranger. It is not thus that the artist creates. All his faculties are set in motion at the same time; in his case, the philosopher, the encyclopedist, the physician, the investigator, all make their appearance together. And, indeed this is necessary, since the materials furnished by all these faculties concur to furnish the actions and words of the character, whom he causes to act and speak. If these were employed by turn and in isolated fashion, the result would be mutilated creatures or abstract beings. With him ideas pile up and crystalize in masses, in every corner of the crucible, according to all the chances and inequalities of inspiration, without symmetrical models and improvised pell-mell; here a glowing phrase that paints a character in foreshortening; next some general maxim, in the same paragraph a flash of sarcasm, a chaos of surging metaphor, reflections and fine sentiments. Your words are a sort of notation, each having its exact value, fixed by root and association; his are symbols whose sense and employment depend upon capricious revery.

He was seven years, he says, learning the French language. The truth is that he studied it profoundly,[1] but in his own way, like others did who are also accused of being barbarians. For such as these a word is not a cipher but an awakener of images; they scan, examine and weigh each word; meanwhile a cloud of emotions and fugitive images floats through their brain; a thousand shades of sentiment, a thousand confused memories, a thousand jumbled glimpses, a bit of melody, a fragment of landscape, entangle each other in their brain; for them the word is the sudden tocsin that summons to the vague

---

[1] See in proof of this the admirable and original style of the "Droll Stories," which resemble the carnations of Jordaëns.

world of vanished dreams. What a distance lies between this kind of sense and that of the grammarians! For it is really a sense; you can not deny it because it escapes you. We are dealing here with a species of architecture, new in truth, but as vast as that of old, which neither imposes its laws upon the latter, nor submits to the latter's laws, and which, like its rival, has its beauties.

First of all grandeur, its richness and novelty. This style is a gigantic chaos; everything is there: the arts, the sciences, the crafts, all history, philosophies, religions; there is nothing which has not furnished it with words. In ten lines you traverse the four corners of thought and of the world. Here is a Swedenborgian idea side by side with a metaphor taken from a butcher or a chemist, two lines further on a philosophic tirade, then a coarse joke, a shade of tenderness, the half-vision of a painter, a bar of music. It is an extraordinary carnival of down-at-the-heel

metaphysicians, Grub-Street Silenuses,
wan scholars, rolicking artists, working-
men in smock-frocks, bedizened and ca-
parisoned with every species of magnificence or frippery, the costumes of every
age elbowing each other, here · tatters,
there golden raiment, purple sewed to
rags, rags edged with brilliants—all this
whirling chaos striving in the dust and
light under the reflection of the gas
lamps with their hard and dazzling glare.
At first all this shocks you; then you become used to it; finally you sympathize
with and enjoy it. Your emotion is stirred by this eruption of strange figures,
this vastness of perspective, this immense
and sudden opening of all horizons. Soon
these queer conceits pique your curiosity;
you take pleasure in an unexpected metaphor; your mind perceives between objects infinitely distant an unexpected link.
The myriad threads by which all things
are joined and held together from one
end of the universe to the other are re-

vealed in this infinitely woven system of network. Chemistry explains love; the kitchen touches elbows with politics; music and grocery are related to philosophy. You see more things and more links between things. Instead of a good-sized and well cultivated garden, we have the enormous and uncertain spoil of a great forest.

Together with the mind the heart is soon moved; under the tumultuous swarming of these engulfing ideas, one feels an increasing warmth. These violent expressions, these heaped-up images of the hospital and the bagnio, this coupling of unheard of terms, the ardor of this style stuffed with ideas that it can hardly contain, proclaim an excess of suffering, of effort and of genius, the like of which never existed. He struggles against the heaviness of his nature and his baggage-load of science; the furnace within him flames up more ardently under the crushing mass, but eventually it will burst. We share in this labor and this victory; we feel the pangs of this fury of obstructed inspiration, of these exploits of a fevered will; but we are dominated by this swelling passion, and this power which triumphs. The impression left is unhealthy, but so strong that we can never forget it. Thus disturbed and carried away, we are no longer astonished at this profusion of images; they pierce through the boiling mass like those red and purple flames that leap from a crucible. He has the eyes of a painter; involuntarily and voluntarily he sees colors and forms; he has need of them; in his case abstractions border upon pictures; in the midst of his reasoning he is diverted by a landscape. I copy his description of a day in the country and of a bouquet; this is what imagination and passion have made of botany.

"Have you ever experienced, in the country fields in the month of May, that perfume which communicates to all living beings a kind of fecund intoxication, which if you are afloat urges you to trail your hand in the wave, to allow your hair to float in the breeze, the while your thoughts re-blossom like forest clusters? A tiny plant, the fragrant *flouve* may be the source of this hidden harmony. No one can wear with impunity such a flower. Mingle in a bouquet, this flower with its striped and radiant petals resembling a robe with white and emerald fillets; and from the depths of your heart will rise a flood of recollections stirring to life the neglected rose in your buttonhole. Place in the bottom of a large porcelain vase some of those white clusters found among the vines of Touraine: vague image of forms beloved, crushed like those of the conquered slave. From this layer mount spirals of rope-weed with white bells, sprigs of red bugrane, mingled with fern and young shoots of oak with lustrous multi-colored leaves, all bending in humble salutation like weeping-willows, timid

and suppliant as prayers. Crowning all
are slender blooming fibrils fluttering in
the breeze, purple amourette shedding its
yellow stamen-tips; snowy pyramids of
meadow-grass culled from field and water, the green hair of the sterile broom;
the fringed plumes of bent grass called
winds-eye; violet esperance, the crown of
virgin dreams, found in the bosom of flax
when the light shines through these
plants abloom. Towering over all are
Bengal roses, clear cut amid the soft gilt
of the daucus, the plumes of the linai-
grette, marabout and meadow-sweet, the
umbels of the wild chervil, the blond hair
of the fruit-bearing clematis, the delicate
and milk-white heraldic cross, the myr-
iad-leaved corymbus, the plenteous stalks
of fumitory with its red and black flowers, the tendrils of the vine, the tortuous
shoots of the honeysuckle; in fine, all that
these naïve things have of abandoned and
disheveled; flames and triple darts, lance-
olated and slashed leaves; stems twined

and twisted like the vague tortured desires in the depths of the heart: from the
bosom of this rich and overflowing tor-
rent of love emerges a trim red poppy
with surrounding buds ready to break
forth, displaying the flame of its sunburst
over starry jasmines and dominating the
incessant shower of pollen—a lovely fluttering cloud in whose glowing mist the
light is reflected. What woman intoxi-
cated by the aphrodisaic perfume hidden
in the heart of the flouve, does not understand that luxury of subdued revery, that
virgin tenderness disturbed by uncon-
quered desires, that flame of passionate
love demanding its due of happiness, and
tho a hundred times refused, renewing
its struggles with unlessened, tireless and
eternal ardor. All that we ever offer to
God—is not all this offered to Love in
this poem of celestial flowers which mur-
murs unceasing music to the heart and
lavishes embraces of veiled voluptuousness, hopes unavowed, which leap up in

flame and then vanish like gossamer dreams on a summer's night."

There is nothing in oriental poetry more dazzling or more magnificent; we have here luxury and intoxication; one seems to bathe in a heaven of perfume and light, and all the voluptuousness of a day in summer takes prisoner the senses and the heart, fluttering and murmuring like a tumultuous swarm of golden butterflies.

It is evident that this man, whatever has been said of him, or whatever he may have done, knows the language, and knows it as well as any one; only he uses it after his own fashion.

CHAPTER IV

THE WORLD OF BALZAC

In his preface of the "Human Comedy," Balzac announces his design of writing the *natural history* of man; his talents were in accord with this design; hence the peculiar physiognomy of his characters; as the father, so the children. When one knows in what manner an artist invents one can foresee his inventions.

In the eyes of the naturalist man is not an independent and superior reasonable being, healthy of himself and capable of attaining by his sole efforts truth and virtue, but a simple force, similar to others in kind, and influenced by circumstances as regards his rank and conduct. He loves this force for itself; he loves it in all its phases, in all its acts; provided that he can see it living he is content. He

163

dissects with equal willingness a pulp or an elephant; he will as willingly resolve into his elements the porter as the prime-minister. For him there is no such thing as ordure. He comprehends and manipulates forces; that constitutes his pleasure; he has no other; he does not say: "the beautiful picture," but "the beautiful subject." And beautiful subjects are curious beings important to science, capable of placing in relief some notable type, some singular deviation from the normal, useful in the explanation of new and far-reaching laws. Purity and grace hardly concern him; in his eyes a toad is the equal of a butterfly; the bat interests him more than the nightingale. If you are of delicate make-up, do not open his book; he will describe things as they are, that is to say, very ugly things, and he will paint them in crude colors without extenuation and without embellishment; if he does embellish, it will be in a strange fashion. As he loves natural forces, and those alone, ·

164

he introduces into his picture the deformities, maladies, and grandiose monstrosities which they produce when magnified.

The ideal is lacking in the naturalist; still more is it lacking in Balzac the naturalist. We have seen that he has none of that vivid and alert imagination by means of which Shakespeare gilds and manipulates the slender threads of human destiny; he is overburdened; we behold him painfully sunken in his scientific dunghill, absorbed in the study of all the fibers of his dissection, encumbered with tools and repulsive preparations: so that when he issues from his cavern and regains the light he exhales the odor of the laboratory in which he has been buried. He lacks true nobility; delicate things escape him; his anatomist's hands pollute modest creatures; he makes ugliness more ugly. But it is in painting baseness that he achieves a triumph. He is at home in the presence of the ignoble, and lives in its atmosphere without repug-

nance; he follows with an inward satis-
faction the bickerings of a household, or
the intrigues of finance. With equal sat-
isfaction he develops his exploits of brute
force. He is armed with brutality and
calculation; reflection has endowed him
with the combinations of wisdom; his
coarseness deprives him of the fear of
shocking his readers. No one is more
capable of describing beasts of prey,
whether small or great.

Such are the limits in which his nature
confines him. He is an artist at once
powerful and ponderous, mastered and
ministered to by the tastes and faculties
of the naturalist. By virtue of this rôle
he copies reality, loves grandiose monsters, and paints better than others baseness and force. Such are the materials
which go to make up his character, which
render some imperfect and others admirable, according as their substance is adapted or unsuited to the mold.

THE WORLD OF BALZAC

I

In the lowest rank are the tradesmen and the provincials. Formerly they were merely grotesque, exaggerated to raise a laugh, or carelessly sketched into some corner of the picture. Balzac describes them seriously; he is interested in them; they are his favorites, and rightly so, for here he is in his own domain. They form the proper subject of the naturalist. They are specimens of society equal to specimens in the natural order. Each one has his instincts, his needs, his defenses, his distinct personality. The occupation produces varieties in man, just as climate produces varieties in the animal; the attitude which it imposes on the soul, being constant, becomes definitive; the faculties and tendencies which it exercises increase in strength; the natural and primitive man disappears; there remains a being, warped but strengthened, formed or de-

167

formed, ugly, but capable of living. This is repulsive, but matters little; these acquired deformities please Balzac's taste. He enters cheerfully into the kitchen, the counting house, or the junk-shop; he does not flinch at any smell or any kind of dirt; his senses are gross. For better or worse he finds himself at ease among· these beings; for there he meets stupidity in full career, vanity of the base and ugly type, but above all self-interest. Nothing here deters him, on the contrary all attracts him. He triumphs in the history of money; it is the grand human motor, especially in these lower depths where men must calculate, heap up, and trick each other on pain of death. Balzac takes part in this thirst for gain, enlists our sympathy in it, embellishes it with the painstaking cleverness of his combinations. His systematized power, his frank love for human ugliness, have created the epic poem of business and finance. Hence his provincial drawing-rooms where creatures dulled by trade or idleness assemble in wrinkled coats and stiff cravats to chat about possible inheritances or the weather, a species of extinguishers under which all ideas perish or grow moldy, prejudice bristles, the absurd plumes itself, cupidity and vain self-love sharpened by long expectation press on by means of a thousand tricks and villainies to the conquest of place or precedence. Hence those state departments where the employees are irritable, brutish, or resigned, some organized to the point of mania, makers of puns and collections, others inert and munching their pens, still others uneasy like monkeys in a cage, full of mystery tho talkative, others shut up in their imbecility like a snail in its shell, satisfied with writing their tasks in a fine, round, irreproachable hand, half starved creatures for the most part, accustomed to roam miry subterraneous depths in order to pocket some gratification or advantage. Hence those shops, spattered by the mud of Paris, deafened by the racket of vehicles, darkened by melancholy, fog and dampness, where lank and feeble little merchants spend thirty years tying up packages, persecuting their clerks, making up inventories, lying and smiling. Hence, above all, those small newspapers, the cruellest of all Balzac's pictures, in whose columns truth, and especially falsehood, is sold, in which thought is doled out at so much an hour, so much a line, "exactly as you light a lamp," whose writers, harassed by want, famished for money, forced to write, treat themselves as machines, treat their art as a trade, despise all things, despise themselves, and find oblivion in orgies of the mind and senses. Hence his prisons, his ordinaries, his Paris, his provincial scenes, and that picture, ever the same tho varied in its details, of human deformity and cupidity. At bottom those things please him; these are his heroes, since it is these that he crowns. Scapin, whom he calls Rastignac, is made a member of the ministry; Turcaret, whom he calls Nucingen, becomes a peer of France and a millionaire thirty times over. The greater part of his knaves wind up by becoming rich, titled, powerful, deputies, public prosecutors, prefects, counts. Gold lace is a sort of aureole, the only one of which they are capable; after the example of society and nature, he places it complacently upon their coat.

II

His men of genius have his genius. Never seek among them that measured and discreet irony which is the natural weapon of reason and good taste, that delicate finesse and propriety of style, that proud and tranquil self-possession that makes the well-bred man sure of his ideas, of his manners, of his position in life. They have a kind of curdled, violent enthusiasm which surges from them, pro-

171

ducing a maelstrom of the trivial and the poetic, the slang of the bank mingled with lyrical imagery, a sort of unhealthy tho powerful intoxication resembling that produced by a fiery, adulterated liquor. They talk like artists and like street gamins, handling everything roughly—philosophy, politics, truth, virtue. Paris has put into their hands all its ideas. They play the blackguard with them after the fashion of sceptics or of children who willingly make fun of the Gospel or the Charter. "You will make your pot boil with an actress who will make you happy; this is what is called a question of state. But to live with a married woman! . . . This is aiming straight at misfortune." And elsewhere: "Do you reproach poor Rastignac for living at the expense of Mme. Nucingen? First of all, speaking in the abstract, as Roger Collard says, the question may be said to concern the *Critique of Pure Reason;* now as regards impure reason . . ." The novel continues thus through two hundred pages; puns, strange and profound ideas, coarse allusions, flamboyant metaphor, sudden caricature suddenly broken off, the blended style of a banker, a preacher, a police commissioner and a painter; their language resembles a Paris garbage barrel, in which is found, pellmell, the débris of extreme wealth and extreme poverty, shreds of lace mingled with cabbage stalks.

That makes a rich soil, I grant you, but grant me that it is infectious. "The effervescence of early youth," says one of his characters, "concealed from my eyes the mechanism of the world; it was necessary to see it, to be bruised by the wheels, to hear the noise of the chains and plates, to be soiled by the grease." Another cries out: "Your jokes are venerable! That story is as well known as a secret remedy!" I pass by still finer examples.

The source of this style is disillusion;

these men have been bruised and made
brazen by experience; they conceive life
as ugly and sordid, and it is with mixed
joy and anger that they throw mud at the
beautiful fabric of enchanting dreams
that appears trembling upon the thresh-
old of youth. Let us add that disen-
chantment takes them by the throat by
assuming its ugliest form, that of the
creditor; bills, protested notes, bailiffs,
seizures are their familiars; their fashion
of talking involuntarily recalls all these;
beyond all their castles in Spain they behold Clichy on the horizon. In order to
put the finishing touch on these melancholy beings, Balzac makes them philosophers; they descant on their century, on
life, on history, bitterly like the van-
quished, or brutally, like tyrants, but always in the style of the misanthropic
viveur who loves to flay mankind and dis-
sect society over a couple of bottles of
champagne. Here is a new kind of diversion peculiar to Paris, to Balzac, and to

the Nineteenth Century—namely, the philosophy of disgust professed in terms of the school and the kitchen in the midst of broken glasses and stamped paper, by half-sick rascal artists who have become demi-financiers.

III

The nature of women is composed of nervous finesse, delicate and alert imagination, and a certain reserve, innate and acquired. That is to say that nearly always it escapes Balzac. At times, I know, his genius as an observer triumphs; he has observed so carefully and reflected so much that he has painted with truth a few virtuous and tender young girls, la Fosseuse, Eveline, Eugénie Grandet, Marguerite Claës. Here and there withal, these chaste figures have stains; but in the others the faults are such that the portrait is utterly spoiled. The man of gross temperament,

175

the pedant philosopher, the physiologist used to the dissecting room, pierces through the badly fastened mask of the virtuous woman. They use the *words of the author*. Mme. Claës, an ignorant Spaniard and housewife, says to her husband, "The life of the soul like physical life has its actions. . . . . Glory is the sunshine of the dead."

Mme. de Mortsauf makes reply to Félix de Vandenesse that she can not love him because of the duty she owes her children and her sick husband: "Has not my confession brought plainly enough before your eyes the three children whom I can never abandon, on whom I ought to shower tears of reparation, and shed rays of sunshine from a soul unstained in the slightest degree." These two women, Mme. Graslin, and many others, were certainly born prophetesses and blue-stockings. Modesty as well as good taste is lacking in them. Modeste Mignon, writing to a young man whom she loves and whom she has seen but once, weeps over the fine gloves "which are the mold of his gentleman's hand." Mme. de Mortsauf, whom the author introduces as a madonna, is guilty of five or six acts that are almost bold, and her last letter lifts high the curtain of the conjugal chamber. The truth is that Balzac enters there too often; no doubt it is necessary to set foot in the toilet chamber after the manner of a chambermaid, or at times to look through the keyhole like a police spy, but if this disenchants, it prevents enchantment. I take no further pleasure in a dainty toilette when I am shown the bill and the way it is put together. I have no more appreciation for a pretty home [1] when I am told the number of basins of fresh water and bottles of vinegar that are necessary to preserve beauty. I have no more admiration for a virtuous woman when, after some good act, I see her pose

---

[1] Ferragus, "Memoirs of Two Young Married Women."

177

like an actress and utter some dramatic rant. When Balzac wishes to paint virtue, religion or love, he degenerates into the heavy bombast of false sublimity, the stiff commonplace of official phraseology, the sensuality of an imagination without shame and of a passionate temperament; his fine portraits of women are elsewhere. They are those poor, grotesque, pretentious, stingy, silly creatures, Mme. Soudry, Mlle. Rogron, Mlle. Gamard, La Grande Nanon, Mlle. Cormon, and a hundred others, deformed by provincial life, by trade, by household cares, bickerings, gossip, their poetry consisting of a mechanical piety, and their ideas of art limited to polishing the furniture, urged on by, and almost feeling the claws of the devil whom their great libertine of a father, Balzac, never fails to whet to his task.

They are also his intriguing women, Mme. Camusot, for example, a kind of panders in petticoats, more cruel and

cunning than the other sort, full of arti-
fice, eager for gain, implacable, more
dangerous than men, because they have
less scruple, less fear and stronger passions. There are still the invalids, Mme.
Graslin, Mme. d'Aiglemont, delicate creatures whom ignorance, chastity and
imagination have made too sensitive, and
who, fallen suddenly into the commonplace of life and the brutalities of marriage, languish, become exalted, are cast
down, and finally fade or perish. Wherever there is any deformity or wound in
question, Balzac is there; he plies his
trade of physiologist; no one has so well
described ugliness and misfortune, and
many praise him for it, claiming that
here is the whole of man.

Marriage, like money, is his armory.
He is always returning to it; it is the
great arsenal of our miseries. In truth,
he wishes to enliven it, and dons his pedant's costume to divert you. He shakes
the tree of science and gives you the

greenest apples to munch. You eat them and you try to laugh, but at bottom you feel like crying. The "Scenes from Married Life" is a masterpiece; but what a sad masterpiece! "You have found your ideal, you! A handsome man, always well groomed, with yellow gloves, well-trimmed beard, polished boots, immaculate linen of the most exquisite propriety, and careful in details." In fact, such is the ideal. "And the promise of happiness, and freedom! One hears the rumble of horses and carriages in his lightest words. Armand gave me the idea of a husband in ermine, of a rich fur robe edged with ostrich plumes in which you are about to wrap yourself." I conclude or rather Cécile de Marville concludes: "Think of giving five hundred thousand francs to her companion in misfortune! Oh, mama! I shall have my carriage and live in the Rue aux Italiens!" The man weds a dowry and respectability, the woman weds a cabriolet

and a fine head of hair. Hence conjugal
bliss of a truly unique species, each having selfish aims, both deceived in their
hopes, using their wits to nag at each
other in secret and to show affection for
each other in public. Piece together all
these vices and forces, and you will have
the blue-stocking and the lorette: Mme.
de Bargeton, Mme. de la Baudraye,
Mme. Schontz, Esther, Josepha, Balzac's
most perfect portraits of women. His
pedantry, his pretentious style, his gran-
diloquent and sweetened phrases, his half
concealed sensuality, are suited to the
blue-stocking who is a courtesan of imagination and who indulges in orgies of the
mind. His audacity, his abandon of style,
his brutal muddy verve, his artist's
nerves, his taste for magnificence and
pleasure, his scientific theory of life and
his cynicism, are suited to the courtesan
who exploits and enjoys the world.

IV

There are, nevertheless, virtuous people in Balzac, for there are such in nature; but his virtuous class is of a peculiar species, and bears, like the others, the earmarks of its author. The poet-moralist, Corneille for example, represents his heroes as upright from the first; they wish to be heroes, they are so; there is no other cause; their will suffices, and suffices of itself to constitute and explain them. The naturalist reasons otherwise; in his view the will has its causes; when a man walks, it is because something impels him; some spring has moved in "the spiritual automaton," and acted upon the physical personality. For him virtue is a product like wine or vinegar, excellent in truth, and something that we ought to have about us in abundance, but

manufactured, like other things, by a
known series of determined operations
having a measurable and certain effect.
Ordinarily it is nothing more than the
transformation or development of some
passion or habit; pride, hardness of mind,
an obedient stupidity, vanity, prejudice,
calculation, are closely related to it; vice
contributes to produce it, just as from
poisonous substances the most precious
perfumes are distilled. The judge, Popinot, is a sort of "little blue mantle," the
systematic and clever benefactor of his
whole neighborhood; but his benevolence
has developed into mania, and you see
that he loves the poor as the gambler
loves his game. The Marquis d'Espard,
having learned that the half of his fortune has come through a criminal confis-
cation that took place two hundred years
ago, discovers the true heir after infinite
pains and turns over his wealth to him,
but we see that his heroic probity has
been nurtured by patrician pride, and

every one divines that what he desires is
to wipe off a stain from his escutcheon.
The lawyer Chesnel sacrifices his fortune,
almost his honor, and saves the family
d'Esgrignon by prodigies of heaped-up
sacrifice. But this zeal is the passion of
an old servant, and the reader discovers
in the blind devotion and ardor of his
love the animal and involuntary fidelity
of a dog. The Pilleraults, the Birotteaus,
are honest through habit and business
pride, through narrowness of mind and
education. Certainly, we can admire them
still; but our admiration dwindles upon
the revelation of the sources of their virtue, all the more because from these
sources flow stupidity and absurdity as
well as beauty. Every moment Birotteau
lets slip the remarks of a perfumer and
simpleton; Pillerault is the dupe of politicians; Popinot lives in sordidness and
reveals the habits of a judicial automaton. Balzac enumerates the stutter-
ings, the warts, the squints, all the petty

misfortunes and all the notable blemishes which are met with in the virtuous man, as in others. All this pictures him clearly, but it brings him down from the skies to earth. He makes him real but smaller. He dwarfs his hero in still another fashion; for he never describes the other sources of virtue, the purest of all, the grandeur of the ideas which sustained Marcus Aurelius, or the delicacy of soul which guided Mme. de Clèves. He has need of hell to encourage his female saints. The benefactions of Bénassis and Mme. Graslin are but the reckoning of a great remorse. Mme. Hulot, Mlle. Cormon, Mme. de Mortsauf make investments at high interest on earth in order to be well paid in heaven. Virtue presented in this light is nothing more than money lent at usury and on pledge. It is the ugliest of Balzac's ideas. Let the naturalist disenchant us; we are resigned to that; but that an artist should suppress in us all elevation and refinement drives us to a revolt, and we are likely to tell him that if he abolishes them in others, it is probably because he does not possess them himself.

V.

In effect, his ideal is elsewhere. His physicians have no greater pleasure than the discovery of some strange or fatal disease; he is a physician, and is like them. On a number of occasions he has described unnatural passions such as can not even be hinted at here.[1] He has painted with infinite detail and with a sort of poetic animation the execrable vermin that swarm and wriggle in the mud of Paris, the Cibots, the Remonecqs, the Mme. Nourissons, the Fraisiers, the poisonous denizens of the dark lower depths, that, magnified by the focussed

---

[1] "The Girl With Golden Eyes," "Sarrasine," "Vautrin," "A Passion in the Desert."

rays of his microscope, exhibit their arsenal of deadly weapons and the diabolic sheen of their infamy. He has gone searching in every secret recess, in every cesspool for strange and unhealthy creatures who live outside the pale of law and nature—gamblers, go-betweens, bohemians, usurers, burglars, spies; he has so successfully penetrated into their inner being, he has so wonderfully balanced and adjusted their springs of action, he has described them so naturally and made their actions seem so logical, that while detesting them, we cannot help admiring them, and, tho the imagination would fain turn away, it can not detach itself from them.

They are, in truth, the heroes of the naturalist and rude artist whom nothing disgusts; they are the curios of his gallery. You pass quickly before his unhandsome virtuous women, his pompous priests, his dull or garrulous would-be great men; real art is not to be found here; a museum is not a *musée*. But you pause before his business men and artisans, each under his glass case exhibiting both the excess and arrest of development which classify it under its species; before his men of talent, all brilliant, perverted and dissatisfied; before his women of the invalid or gossip type, his authoresses, his lorettes; before his honorable men, prepared like the others according to his sorry anatomical method, whose virtues are born of their prejudices, their hobbies, their vile habit of calculation or their vices; before those deformed or eccentric beings which he holds in reserve and places in high relief as special attractions. Be patient for a moment; he is going to lift the curtain and you will see in a hall apart, the monsters of the huge species; he loves them still more dearly than the pygmies.

CHAPTER V

THE GREAT CHARACTERS

If you believe that reason is the essential thing in human nature, you will take reason for your hero, and you will paint generosity and virtue. If your eyes are directed to the external machine, and are fixed merely upon the body, you will choose the body for your ideal, and you will paint voluptuous flesh and muscular vigor. If you regard sensibility as the important part of man, you will see beauty only in lively emotions, and you will picture great sorrows and delicate sentiments.[1] Your conception of nature will influence your conception of beauty; your idea of the real man will suggest to you the ideal man; your philosophy will direct your art. It is thus that Balzac's philosophy has directed Balzac's art. He con-

---

[1]Examples: Corneille, Rubens, Dickens.

189

sidered man a force; he has taken force for his ideal. He has freed it from its fetters, he has painted it in its completeness, free, released from the bonds of reason which prevent it from injuring itself, indifferent to the laws of justice which prevent it from injuring others; he has magnified it, mastered it; exploited it and put it on exhibition as worthy of the first rank; he has crowned it as hero and sovereign in the realm of monomania and villainy.

How can folly and vice be made beautiful? How can our sympathy be won for beasts of prey and diseased brains? How is it possible to negate the almost universal dictum of all literatures, and declare interesting and grand the very things upon which they have heaped ridicule and odium? What is there more disgraceful than the gross trooper, the mark for gibes and the subject for misadventures, from Plautus to Smollet? Observe how he can be transformed; Bal-

zac explains how; you will perceive the
reason for his vices; you will realize their
power and take an interest in seeing them
in action. You are fascinated by the logic
of it all, and one-half of your disgust and
mortification disappears.

Philip Brideau is a soldier, depraved
by the family trade, by misfortune, by
success. An officer at eighteen, his education was received at first in the Wa-
terloo campaign, and amidst the trea-
sons of the disbanded army; later in
Texas amidst scenes of American selfishness and brutality. A lieutenant-colonel
and twice decorated, he is flung from the
highest pinnacle of youthful dreams, ambition, success, into the midst of his
ruined family, a poor wretch, pursued
and suspected, shut up like a lion behind
the wire grating of a cage, or a shame-
less prowler in the lower depths of the
theater or the newspaper office, often ill
from debauchery wallowed in for the
sake of oblivion or distraction finally ap-

prehended as a conspirator against the state and thrown into prison as he is leaving the hospital. He has been hardened by the sight and the exercise of force, his wits have been sharpened by the humiliation of defeat and the privations of poverty; he has been corrupted by association with knaves, by accustomed drunken orgies, by the indulgence of his family, by his mother's adoration, by impunity for his first crimes. Are you astonished now if he makes a parade of his practical contempt for justice and mankind?

The mind is caught in the current of these causes as in a river. We no longer shrink from the gross habits of Philip, we want to see them; his character has need of them and makes us need them. Furthermore, their atrociousness retrieves them; by reason of his callousness he becomes great. There is no longer anything human in his nature; he exploits everything and tramples on everything. Having flown from his cage, he frightens his mother by threatening suicide; they embrace him, weep over him and offer him on their knees all the family possessions. "That will do," said he, "the announcement has had its effect." Here is gratitude. He has cheated out of her last cent the aged Descoing, his second mother, and on the morrow found her dying; hear him: "You would drive me away, wouldn't you? Oh, yes! You would like to play the melodrama of 'The Prodigal Son.' Come, come! So this is the way you are going to act? Well, you are a pretty lot of cocoanuts. What have I done wrong? I have cleaned up a paltry mattress that belongs to the old lady. Tell me, in the name of the fiends, was there any money inside it? Well, here is some." This is the way he repents.

He has been fed and cared for by a companion in arms and debauchery, named Giroudeau; when he becomes prosperous he deserts his benefactor; "he has no manners," said Philip. This is his idea of friendship. To acquire a million francs he marries a woman of low origin; he takes her to Paris and throws her into the demi-monde, then into the lowest sinks of vice, and finally leaves her to die of misery and disease. This is how he keeps his marriage vow. He has killed his mother by the brutal character of his ingratitude. A comrade sent by the family beseeches him to come to the death-bed. He begins to laugh: "What in the devil's name should I do there? The only service that the good woman can render me is to collapse as soon as possible. I am an old camel that has forgotten how to genuflect. Mother wishes, apropos of her last sigh, to aim a carrot at me on my brother's account. Thanks." Such is his filial affection. Who thinks any longer of the unbridled grossness of the libertine and soldier. Here infamy is drowned in horror; it is the inhuman and sinister brilliance of a brazen image.

THE GREAT CHARACTERS

Balzac supplements all this with strength. The education which has perverted Philip has clothed him in steel armor; a cutthroat and gambler in the hazards of war and roulette, he has acquired that sangfroid which gives a man self-possession and mastery over others. He has a "glance that crushes fools," dissimulation which deceives every one, and an eye that seizes opportunity. Observe with what fine style, with what haughtiness and contempt, with what guard-house gravity he indoctrinates his uncle, an old imbecile at the mercy of his servant and her lover: "Good day, gentlemen," addressing visitors, "I am taking a walk with my uncle, as you see, and I am trying to form him, for we live in an age when children are obliged to undertake the education of their grandparents. . . . I will kill Maxence for you like a dog. In place of him you shall take me home with you, and I will have this pretty girl appear before you in broad daylight. Yes,

by God's thunders! Flora shall love you!
Or, if you are not satisfied with her, I
will horsewhip her. . . . You will live
together like hearts in orange blossoms
after the time of mourning is past; she
will wriggle like a worm, she will squall,
and finally she will be dissolved in tears.
Let the water flow, however."

Never has cynicism and disdain found
expression more bitter, more poignant.
Philip draws blood and beats men as tho
they were cattle, after the manner of a
Cossack or a butcher. He is so strong
that he squanders strength. He makes
the sword leap from the hand of Maxence, tells him to pick it up again, and
having thus insulted him by first sparing
him, kills him. He is as great a sharper
as he is a duellist, and succeeds in pocket-
ing his uncle's property; he then disen-
cumbers himself of his uncle, his wife,
his friends, and his mother, installs himself in the public favor by wearing the
outward garb of a man of honor and

generous sentiments, wins the cross, a title, millions, and reaches the pinnacle of success. In order to put the finishing touches upon him Balzac has endowed him with the philosophy of vice; a villain is never perfect unless his villainy is based on principle; it is essential that he appreciate his own worth and understand what he does; he must glory in his work, call cruelty justice, insult alike virtue and mankind, justify his crimes by the authority of reason, reduce crime to a set of maxims and exhibit it in an aureole of reason under the light of heaven. Impudence and philosophy are the crowning traits. Listen to Philip: "Women are bad children; they are animals, inferior in nature to men, and it is necessary to make them fear him; for the worst condition for us is to be governed by those brutes." And elsewhere: "I am but an upstart, my dear. I do not like my rough edges to be seen! My son, here, will be more fortunate than I; he will be a great lord. The wag will wish for my death; indeed, I shall expect that, for otherwise he would not be my son."

You see that he does himself justice, and settles down into his brutality as into a splendid and comfortable bed. Machiavelli or Borgia could not have said better. What matter his end and the two or three strokes of fortune that ruined and killed him? A stone may fall into the finest machine, break some spring and thus disorganize the whole; the machine remains none the less a masterpiece. What tho it grind and tear, we do not think of that; we only think of the geometrical combinations of its steel wheel-work, of the formidable grinding teeth, of its mighty gearing, of the wonderful flight of the shuttle appearing and vanishing in a flash, of the mournful gleam of the crunched iron which glitters and groans; the artist has conquered me, has carried me away, dazzled me, and I know no more and desire no more than to admire him.

This trooper could still be made poetic; he has boldness and phlegm, and Balzac had but to parade these qualities to accomplish his design. But what can be done with a miser? What is there great in a grimy, shriveled, palsied usurer, accustomed to keeping accounts and nibbling profit from the goods of others. Is it possible to write on this theme after Molière, and even to contradict Molière? What is Harpagon but a grotesque creature whom the poet exaggerates and libels for the purpose of amusing or correcting us? Count all his ridiculous qualities; can you find a place where beauty may find lodgment? His stinginess is the more infamous because he has been born a rich bourgeois, and his station in life obliges him to have servants, carriages and jewelry. What is there viler than a usurer mounted on his coach, inventing cheap dishes, a hoarder up of candle ends and a rent collector? He is railed at by his neighbors, vilified by his servants; he allows his son to plunge into debt and his daughter to run away; he lends on pawn and loses; he hides his money and has it stolen; he wishes to marry and is robbed of his mistress; he tries to be gallant and becomes imbecile; he weeps and the spectators laugh. What methods to render a character grotesque! Now by adopting the contrary methods we may make the character romantic; the ridiculous and base creature becomes tragic and grand. Harpagon turned inside out becomes Grandet. Let us make him a peasant, a cooper, a pruner of vines; his smallness becomes excusable; if he counts the lumps of sugar at breakfast, if he nails up his nephew's casks, if he calls his servant before him to tell her how to save a candle, it is because early habits last, because the youth persists in the old man, and the mind always retains its first impressions; we should have done as much in his place, and we tolerate this avarice which in another would shock us.

THE GREAT CHARACTERS

Harpagon, awkward, mocked and duped, is a subject for laughter; Grandet, clever, honored and happy, becomes an object of fear. He exploits his kindred, his family, his friends and his enemies. He has for a servant a female rustic with the cut of a grenadier, whom no one likes, whom he has imbued with a machine-like devotion to his interests and the fidelity of a beast of burden. For his wife he has chosen a devotee who is a thrifty housekeeper, a slave to her religious duties, delicate minded and imbecile, who lets him hoard up to his heart's content and never asks him for a sou. He has brought up his daughter in strict economy, and profited by her filial virtue to deprive her of her rightful inheritance. He gets rid of his ruined nephew, and finds the means to do the generous thing by him by taking his jewels at a Jew's price. He is respected by the richest bourgeois, who pay court to him in the hope of marrying his daughter. He abstracts from them dozens of favors, receiving from one gratuitous advice, sending another to Paris to look after his business. He profits by all passions, by all virtues, by all misfortunes; he is a veritable diplomat, an obstinate calculator, so attentive and so prudent that he dupes professional business men and beats lawyers at their own game. He commenced with two hundred louis and ended with seventeen millions. The splendor of gold here covers the ugliness of vice, and glorified avarice seats itself upon success as upon a throne.

To lift it still higher, Balzac equips it with all the strength of genius and will. Grandet is so superior a man that ordinarily he consents to play the ignorant and humble blockhead; he stutters, complains of headache, says that he can not understand the complications of business; as a result his rivals are thrown off their guard and deliver over to him their secrets. He laughs in his sleeve at them, he amuses himself by making them run and sweat for him, he makes a plaything of their expectation and their fawnings: "Enter, gentlemen," says he to his visitors, tufted city gentry. "I am not proud." And he makes them be seated beside his servant in the light of a tallow candle. He installs himself in his avarice as Brideau does in his brutality. He bristles with maxims of atrocious precision and convincing power. When his brother is killed and his nephew weeps, he says, "We shall have to excuse the first shower; but this young man is good for nothing, he takes more interest in dead men than in money." Do you laugh at a man who uses such words? This utterance is like a knife which cuts away at a stroke the roots of humanity and pity. The vice of the man is a dogma embraced with the eagerness of the heart's desire and the passion of love. At home he is a tyrant and terrible; the women tremble under his glance; they are his "linnets," frail little animals to whom he gives from time to time a few grains of wheat, but whose necks he might twist at any time with a movement of his thumb. Anger rumbles in his crude and sarcastic outbursts: "I will not give you *my* money to trap this young fool with sugar. What! More candles? The wenches would tear up the floors of my house to cook eggs for this gallant!"

We are carried away by the vehemence of his flaming anger; you perceive that this access of vice has neither bridle nor measure, that it breaks all, tramples all, outrages the sentiments and happiness of others; it is like a bull rushing headlong through a church. "What good does it do you to feed upon the good God (*manger le bon Dieu*) twice a month, if you secretly give your father's gold to a good-for-nothing who will devour your very heart when you have nothing else to give him?" His wife adjures him in the name of God. "What the devil does your good God amount to?" says he. At this

point one fears for human nature; you
feel that it conceals unknown gulfs capable of swallowing up everything—the
paternal instinct, religion itself!

When his daughter signs the paper in
which she renounces her mother's inheritance, he turns pale, breaks out into a
sweat, almost collapses, and then embraces her to the point of suffocation.
"Ah, my child! You give life to your
father. That is the way business ought
to be done. Life is business. I bless you.
You are a virtuous daughter, and you
love your father well." This smallness,
this blessing granted as wages due, these
sudden half-strangled cries of the miser
overwhelming the father, are horrible.
At this height, and accompanied by these
actions, passion reaches the level of poetry; and perhaps such a miser is in truth
a poet, spoiled and in obscurity. In imagination he swims in a river of gold.
He speaks of his treasure in the lively
and caressing style of a lover and an art-

ist. "Come, fetch it hither, the little darling! You ought to kiss me on the eyes for telling you the life and death secrets of the crown-pieces. In truth, the crowns live and move like men: this goes, that comes, that one sweats, that one earns." Having ended, his eyes rest for whole hours upon piles of louis as though he were being warmed in their sunshine. "That warms me," he says.

Do you still find this grotesque? What joys this man has tasted! He has spread his sails like a poet amid the hopes and discoveries of a hundred thousand fairy-lands of splendor; he has tasted the continuous, long-drawn-out pleasures of increasing success, of repeated victory, of conscious superiority, of established mastery. He has not suffered in the affections, in money-matters, or from privation or remorse; he dies at the extreme limit of old age, in possession of his wealth and in security, completely satiated by his master passion, all other de-

206

sires being eradicated or extinguished. If Corneille has produced the noble epic of heroism, Balzac has created the triumphant epic of passion.

· These two characters escape ugliness by reason of their strength; let us choose a passion which constitutes weakness; instead of a beast of prey let us take a fool; let us seek out a vice which makes its victim not a tyrant but a slave, and which devours the heart and the life of the victim, instead of ravaging the life and happiness of others. There is one such, the most bemocked of all, the common laughing stock of ancient and modern comedy—the libertinism of an amorous old man whose fate it is to be duped, robbed and then thrown aside. This type also becomes a hero in Balzac's hands, for what matters the man to him? Is it Grandet or Brideau that interests me? What are they in the artist's eyes but a mere pedestal on which to sculpture passion? That is what he admires, for that is what is grand, eternal, sovereign, the devastator of nature and of the human race. Its power is the same and equally visible when it shatters the objects surrounding it or the vessel which contains it. It is a fine thing to see passion enter like a poison into a healthy and vigorous body, inflame its blood, twist its muscles, toss it in somersaults, beat it down, and then slowly undermine the inert mass that it never lets out of its grasp.

Baron Hulot d'Ervy, one of the great administrators of the Empire, almost minister, father of a most flourishing family, adored by the most beautiful and virtuous of women, a man of talent, originality, experience and resolution, generous and amiable by nature, allows himself, little by little, to be infected with this poison. Opera girls have devoured his fortune; he has no more money to support his family and give his daughter a marriage portion, and his passion, grown by constant habit, has become an obsession. "And all this for a woman who deceives me, who makes fun of me when I am not by, and who calls me an old *dyed cat!* Oh! it is frightful to think that vice should cost more than what would feed a family. And it is irresistible! I might promise you now not to return to this abominable Jewess; if she were to write me two lines I should go back as one goes into fire under the Emperor!" A vice thus enrooted becomes monomania. The opium smoker who sees his comrade gasping in the corner of the tavern says: "That is how I shall be in three months," and refills his pipe; by a law foreseen and irrevocable, passion seizes the man in its iron jaws and draws him into the infamous and sordid rut of complete shame and misery. Dismissed by his song-bird, Hulot falls in love with a pretty woman who seems to be honest, the most dangerous courtezan ever painted, equal to Shakespeare's Cleopatra, a queen in her audacity, an artist in pas-

sion and originality. In this gulf is swal-
lowed the débris of his fortune. He
pledges his honor, signs notes of hand,
sells his credit, leaves his wife without
bread, sends his uncle, an honest peasant,
as obedient as a soldier, to pillage his
African remittances. By degrees, the
prudent father, the administrator, the
man of honor, disappear in the de-
bauchee. Vice mounts up in him like a
sea, drowning humanity, common sense
and honor. In the midst of all this dis-
aster, he discovers that his mistress is
deceiving him for two rivals; she, herself, tells him this to his face, in a sudden burst of independence and insolence.
He pleads for pardon, the wretch! He
consents to find a place for her husband;
he recognizes the child; nay, more, he
believes himself beloved and melts with
tenderness; his eyes are clouded, he
drinks shame without minding it any
more; possessed by a fixed idea, he perceives nothing else; he goes straight

THE GREAT CHARACTERS

ahead like a child who has his eyes fixed
on some desired fruit and stumbles along
through mud and brambles; he is hardly
disabused when the pair of sharpers discover his adultery and thereby extort the
last remnant of his property and credit.
At the same moment the mountain of
misfortunes piled up by his vices crum-
bles and overwhelms him in a single
shock. His son totters under the weight
of promissory notes; his wife, dragged to
the verge of dishonor by the extremes of
despair and by her sublime self-sacrifice,
is in a dying condition; his aged brother,
an austere republican, dies after a three
days' illness; his uncle, imprisoned on his
account, commits suicide in his cell by
means of a nail. Thunderstruck by the
contempt of the prince, his patron, driven
from his places, declared a thief, he sinks
"almost annihilated" by the wreck of the
fortunes he has ruined, the tears of the
families that he has dishonored, the
knell of two deaths caused by him. Is

211

this enough? Will physiological romance pause before this death-agony of honor? Logic leads it still further; to the very end mighty convulsions are the heralds of dissoluteness and death. Henceforth Hulot is not a man, but "a mere temperament." Delicacy, elegance, love, all that can embellish or excuse vice, is annihilated for him; there remain mere habit and appetite. He sinks to the depth of borrowing money from the singer, his old mistress. He lives with grisettes, quitting one after the other, "like a novel one has read," among barroom drunkards, supernumeraries, paid applauders, the most unclean canaille, himself worthy of the knaves he meets, always pursued and in debt, winding up by becoming a public writer in a stall, having bought with a little money and burnt almonds a poor innocent child of fifteen. His degradation is transformed into idiocy; he degenerates into a species of instinct, machine-like and physical. Found again by his wife, who desires to restore to him his family and his wealth, he says to her, "I am very willing, but can I bring along the little girl?" It is the blind and horrible instinct of a famished wretch who gropes after and hangs on to his last crust. As a climax he is smitten with a coarse woman from Normandy, an ill-shaped kitchen wench. "My wife has not long to live," says he to her, "and if you wish, you may be a baroness." This remark reaching his poor, sick wife actually kills her, and the kitchen maid becomes a baroness. What a speech and what a finale! What an ensemble and climax! Lucretius has produced nothing more powerful, not even when, with the enthusiasm of despair and unrelenting logic, he describes the plague of Athens, and lifts it to the plane of the epic.

Let us pause here; from these three portraits one may judge of the others. Balzac, like Shakespeare, has painted villains of every species, those of the world and of Bohemia, those of finance and of politics,[1] lechers and spies.

Like Shakespeare, he has described monomania in all its varieties; that of licentiousness and avarice, of ambition and science, of art, of paternal love, of passion.[2] Endure in one what you endure in the other. We are not dealing here with practical and moral life, but with imaginary and ideal life. Their characters are spectacles, not models; greatness is always beautiful, even in misfortune and crime. No one asks you to approve them or follow their example. You are only asked to behold and admire. In the open country I much prefer to

---

[1]Vautrin, Mme. Marneffe, de Marsay, Nucingen, Philippe Brideau, La Palferine, Maxime de Trailles, etc. Compare with these: Richard III., Iago, Lady Macbeth, Macbeth, Regan, Goneril, etc.

[2]Claës, Hulot, Grandet, Goriot, Louis Lambert, Marcas, Frauenhofer, Sarrasine, Facino Cane, etc. In Gambara and Massimilla Doni, a small novel in two parts, there are seven kinds of monomania.

Compare, Coriolanus, Hamlet, Lear, Othello, Antony, Hotspur, Juliet, Posthumus, Timon.

meet a sheep than a lion; but from behind cage-bars I vastly prefer a lion to
a sheep. Art is just this sort of cage;
by eliminating fear, interest is attained.
Henceforth, without suffering and without danger, we may contemplate superb
passions, gigantic struggles, lacerations,
all the tumult and strength of human nature bursting its bounds in combats
without pity and desires without limit.
And certainly their contemplated force
moves and attracts. It lifts us beyond
ourselves; we soar beyond the vulgar
sphere of our little faculties and timid
instincts. Our souls expand before this
spectacle and these contrasts; we feel as
we do in the presence of Michael Angelo's wrestlers, those terrible statues
with their enormous distended muscles
which seem to menace with destruction
the pigmies who gaze at them; and we
understand how these two mighty artists
dwell in a kingdom of their own, far
from the public domain, in the fatherland
of art.

BALZAC—A CRITICAL STUDY

Shakespeare has found more striking words, more extravagant deeds, more despairing cries; he has more enthusiasm, more madness, more fire; his genius is more natural, more abandoned, more violent; he invents by instinct, he is a poet; he sees and makes us see by sudden illuminations the abysms and the farthest reach of things, like those grand lightning flashes seen in southern nights which reveal and light up with flame the whole horizon.

Balzac slowly lights and stirs up his furnace; we feel pain at his efforts; we partake of his painful labors in the black and smoky workshops where he prepares, by scientific means, thousands of lanterns, which he arranges in infinite variety so that their intermingled and united rays light up the whole country. At the end all embrace; the spectator looks; he sees less suddenly, less easily, less splendidly with Balzac than with Shakespeare, but he sees the same things, on as large a plane.

CHAPTER VI

BALZAC'S PHILOSOPHY

The test of a superior mind is the conception of the whole. This is, at bottom, the supreme test; the other gifts but serve to prepare the way for the manifestation of this; if it is wanting, the others remain mediocre; without a philosophy, the savant is but a workman, the artist but an entertainer. Hence, the high rank of Ampère in physics, of Geoffroy Saint-Hilaire in zoology, of M. Guizot in history. Hence also Balzac's rank among novelists.

I

He had general ideas on everything, so much so that his books are encumbered with them and their beauty suffers from them. The causes, consequences and

217

alignments of each faculty and each passion, the effects on the character, private
or public, of each condition, and of each
profession, how one makes or under-
mines his fortune, the hundred thousand
truths relative to man and men which go
to make up the experience of life—all this
is in his works; there are treatises on
marriage, business, banking, failure, public office, the family, the press. He phil-
osophizes and his characters philosophize
at every instant. This abundance of
thought is what makes his characters
great; nearly always their words are
worth meditating upon. · Each one comes
upon the stage with a mass of reflections
accumulated during a long life; and all
these masses, contrasting and interrelated, constitute in their union and their
contrast the encyclopedia of the world
of society.

What is the world, and what are the
forces that guide it? In the eyes of Balzac the naturalist, they are the passions

and self-interest. Politeness adorns them, hypocrisy disguises them, shallowness clothes them with fine names; but, at bottom, out of ten actions, nine spring from egotism. And there is nothing surprising in this, for in the grand pell-mell each one trusts in himself; the constant thought of the animal is to sustain and defend himself; and the animal persists in man, with this difference, that the mind of man being vaster, his wants and his perils are greater. This is why Balzac regards society as a conflict of egotisms, where force guided by cunning triumphs, where blind and violent passion forces the dikes which we oppose to it, where the accepted morality consists in apparent respect for convention and for the law. This melancholy and dangerous view of life is enhanced by the fact that he fashions his men of genius out of criminals, that in laying down the theory of vice he makes it unconsciously interesting and excusable, that he paints

in dull colors elevated and refined sentiments, while he portrays admirably the
emotions of gross and base natures, and
that from time to time, carried away by
his subject, he throws out maxims contrary to the public security and possibly
alarming to the sense of honor.[1] Besides,
this acrid philosophy lacks its natural
counterpoise, history, which he knew
badly; he forgot that if, at the present
time, man exhibits many vices and miseries, in former times he exhibited still
more, that increased experience has
minimized the extravagance of the imagination, the blindness of superstition, the

[1]"Virtuous people nearly always look upon their case
with some suspicion; they think that they have been
fooled in the great mart of life."—*The Poor Relations.*

"He was ignorant of the fact that at twenty-six, the
period when a man has formed his judgment of man,
social interests and relations, the opinions for which
he has sacrificed his future, should be modified in his
case as in the case of all truly superior men."—*The Old
Maid.*

"He saw the world as it is, the laws and the moral
impotence of the rich, and he saw in wealth the *ultima
ratio mundi.—Father Goriot.*

heat of passion, the brutality of manners, the intensity of suffering, and that each century sees an increase in our knowledge and our power, our moderation and our security. To philosophize on man exact observation is not enough; what is required is complete observation; and the picture of the present does not represent the history of the past.

For as soon as one has considered what the past was, he is tempted to regard the present as noble and honorable. In truth nothing is more deceptive than the words, beauty and goodness; nothing is more dangerous than to employ them in judging the world. One should never say that the world is bad, or the contrary. Thus employed, these words signify that things are beautiful or ugly by comparison with certain other things; that is why, if you compare them with different objects, these same things will assume a contrary name and quality. The truth is that in the world there is a meas-

ure of good which appears great if compared to the least, small if compared to
the greatest, and which, as in the case of
all quantity, is neither great nor small in
itself. You find a man vile and bad; that
is because you bear in your soul the
image of a just and happy life, and com-
paring your life with that other you perceive its vast superiority. But if you
consider life in its natural and animal
state, the unbridled and discordant play
of imagination and desire, the necessary
conflict between the world and the will,
you will wonder at the proportion of justice and goodness that subsists amidst
these storms, and you will praise the
noble quality in human nature which in
the midst of so many blind and unleashed
forces preserves and redeems reason and
virtue. So that, according to this view
and at will, a man may appear virtuous
or vicious, beautiful or ugly, fortunate or
miserable, without one of these terms ex-
plaining his true nature, without one of

these words determining a rule of life or conduct; and this is explained by the fact that each one of these terms merely measures the distance between a real being and a certain being of the imagination that you create arbitrarily, that you magnify or minimize at your pleasure, and that may vary in every sense *ad infinitum*. Avoid these vague terms if you would treat of morality or politics; endeavor by means of history and experience to understand things. In a given number of actions reckon up how many are selfish and how many generous; the proportion established, you will know in what extent peace and war enter into the present constitution of society, and you will be able to consult the interests of yourself and others. Analyze and ponder the propensities and dominant qualities of your race and your age; this distinction established, you will recognize the leading forces of your country and understand what kind of government they demand and can abide. Otherwise you will write, like Rousseau or M. de Maistre, influenced by passionate emotions and abstract theories, concluding absolutely in favor of a republic or a despotism, according to the optical illusion which has been the misleading guide of Balzac.

His theory of morality, in fact, gives birth to his political system. Like all those who have a bad opinion of mankind he is an absolutist.[1] When one sees nothing in society but passions naturally egoistic and hostile to one another, one cries out for a strong arm to bridle and control them. Thus did Hobbes, the theorist of despotism, who, at the outbreak of the English revolution, cried out for rods of iron and a tamer of beasts to deal with the destructive animals who had slipped their chains. Balzac detests and despises our democratic society, and on every possible occasion he breaks out

---

[1] See the "Country Doctor," the "Village Priest," the "House of Nucingen," the General Preface, etc.

in reproaches, often brutal, against the
government and the Chambers. He de-
plores the failure of Charles the Tenth's
coup d'état, "the most farseeing and salu-
tary measure that a monarch ever adopted for the happiness of his people." He
thinks that a government is strong in
proportion as "it looks to the establishment of a limited *privileged class;*" that
"the principle of suffrage is one of the
most fatal principles of modern government;" that "the proletariat is the undermining principle of a nation and should
always be kept in tutelage." He regrets
the passing away of the hereditary peer-
age and primogeniture. "The great
weakness of France is the law of inheritances in the Civil Code, which provides
for the division of wealth in equal
shares." He regards as ridiculous the
abolition of the lottery, a sort of opium
which helped the people to endure their
misery; the establishment of savings-
banks which encouraged servants to rob

their masters; the institution of courses of study which ruined many fine minds and manufactured a multitude of learned fools. He put his ban upon the freedom of the press, and called newspapers "magazines of poison." There are not enough such despotic institutions to satisfy him, and he thinks there should be added to all these fine things a few trifles taken at random. "The laws," says one of his favorite politicians, "are spiderwebs through which the large flies pass, and which catch the small ones."

"What would you advocate, then?"

"An absolute government, the only one able to punish the crimes of the intellect. Yes, arbitrary law saves the people by coming to the rescue of justice."

As a climax he adds to the tyranny of the state religious tyranny. He desires one for the mastery of the mind, the other for the mastery of the body. "Instruction, or rather education, by the religious bodies is the great life-principle of the people, the only means of diminishing the total of evil and of augmenting the total of good in society. Thought, the principle of evil and of good, can only be cared for, molded, directed, by religion."

It is clear that with the police on one side and Hell on the other, one may do much with mankind, and that a people deprived of equality by an aristocracy, of liberty by a despotism, of thought by the Church, would be too happy to bother about getting enough to eat, and would be satisfied if they were not beaten too hard. Ill furnished minds may perhaps reply to you that you seek your remedy against the vices of men in a man naturally as vicious as others and spoiled, to boot, by the license of absolute power. They may call your attention to the fact that if a free press and parliament are the arena of rival ambitions and the organs of selfish interests, they give a hearing to minorities against tyrannous majorities, and that in times of urgent need

public opinion makes them rally perforce
to the standard of truth and right. They
would point out that if man is bad, his
very vices can supply their own bridle,
and that pride in England, well understood selfishness in the United States, can
maintain public peace and prosperity better than has ever been acomplished by
the despotism of a Church or king. They
might add that a good politician does not
oppose invincible tendencies, that a certain vanity and spirit of justice have im-
planted in France the doctrine of equal
rights and equal sharing of goods; that
the increase of wealth, leisure and
education will give to the country a scientific administration of public affairs; in
brief, that the fire can not be prevented
from burning, and that it is the part of
wisdom to regulate and utilize the flame.
They would conclude that on the subject
of politics, as upon other subjects, Balzac
has produced a romance.

He has produced many of them, nota-

bly in the field of psychology and metaphysics. In order to discover truth in
the region of great ideas, it is necessary
to distrust one's self, to retrace one's steps
a hundred times, to verify one's conjec-
tures every moment, to know how to ig-
nore many things, to separate seeming
truths from certitudes, to weigh carefully
the probable, and to advance with method
in the broad path already tested by analysis and experiment. Every philosopher
contains a sceptic. Balzac was that neither by nature nor vocation. His nature
and his vocation oblige him to imagine
and to believe, for the observation of the
romancist is nothing more than divination; he does not perceive sentiments as
the anatomist perceives fibers; he conjec-
tures them from gestures, physiognomy,
habits, environment, and so vividly that
he seems to touch them, no longer know-
ing how to distinguish direct and certain
cognition from indirect and doubtful
knowledge.[1] His instrument is intuition,

---

[1] Louis Lambert, "Theory of Intuition."

a superior tho dangerous faculty, by
means of which a man imagines or discovers in an isolated fact the entire series
of facts which have produced it, or which
are destined to produce it—a kind of second sight proper to prophets and som-
nambulists who at times hit upon the
truth, tho often upon falsehood, and
who ordinarily attain only seeming truth.
Balzac employs it in the sciences; you
shall judge with what effect. When per-
ceptions are kept, one by one, under the
control of experience, they express the
nature of the things that they represent;
but when they develop of themselves, and
solely of themselves, they merely express
the nature of the mind which forms them.
If this mind is clear, dry, incapable of
seizing the whole of things, they will be
materialistic. If it is vague, poetic, inclined to abstraction, they will be mysti-
cal. Thus are born nearly all the great
systems of religion and philosophy.
Hence the dreams of several great poets

of the present day, this one copying
Pythagoras and believing that pebbles
are concentrated souls, another imitating
the school of Alexandria and soaring in
the mirage of a Christianity only half
Christian. Thus thought and dreamed
Balzac, creating the world and the soul
out of the fabric of his own imagination.
As that imagination was a trifle gross
and accustomed to give a body to invisible things, he could not contemplate ideas
as they are and in their native purity; he
pretended that the soul is a fluid, a kind
of etherized matter analogous to electricity; "that the brain is an alembic in
which are contained certain animal forces
which are absorbed by the various organ-
isms and transformed into will;" that our
sentiments and feelings are simply movements of this fluid; that it "spurts forth"
in anger; that it weighs heavily upon our
nerves in expectation; "that the current
of this king of fluids under the high
pressure of thought and feeling now

231

bursts forth in a flood, now shrinks to a
thin stream, now gathers its forces in a
sort of water spout." He believed that
"ideas are complete and organized beings,
having their existence in the invisible
world, and wielding an influence over
our destinies;" that, concentrated in a
powerful brain, that of a hypnotist for
example, they obtain a mastery over the
brain of others, and are able to overleap
in an instant enormous intervals of time.
He thus explains the transmission of
thought, distant visions, prophetic divination, nerve insensibility, the power of
the muscles, the perfecting of the senses,
the cure of diseases, apparitions, possessions, catalepsies, ecstasies, and all those
strange or doubtful facts that the occult
sciences tell us of, and that unrecognized
sciences are to-day trying to rehabilitate.
He also explained many other things,
constructing his theories ably and clev-
erly, heaping up documents, and ably
linking together his facts, but involun-

tarily weakening his theories by blending
with them so much of imagination and
poetic conception. "The pleasure of bath-
ing in a lake of pure water, in the midst
of rocks, of woods and flowers, alone and
caressed by a warm breeze, will give a
very feeble image of the happiness that I
experienced when my soul was bathed in
waves of ineffable light, when I heard
the voices of inspiration, terrible and confused, when from an unknown source I
felt a flood of visions in my palpitating
brain."

It is not thus that the laws of psychology are discovered; there is needed more
calm and circumspection. In this tempest all is counfounded; light, sound,
ideas, the visible and the invisible world;
you see nothing beyond a subtle and
resplendent phantasmagoria; you are dis-
posed, like Louis Lambert, to regard
thought as a kind of flame, and the forces
of the universe as a species of ether. In
the thirteenth century when poets, vision-

aries and the demented swarmed, we see the Manicheans holding that God is a brilliant and subtle liquid impregnating matter, after the manner of a sponge. Happily, we are no longer in the age of the Manicheans.

These materialists became mystics readily. Balzac was both and for the same reason.[1] The tranquil deductions of the savant are distasteful to these tumultuous and poetic minds; they appear to them sluggish, cold and impotent; they much prefer to abandon themselves to the magnificent raptures and lightnings of the storms that rage in their bosoms. They conclude by believing in the reality of these and regarding them as a superhuman power of divination, which is alone capable of revealing to man the infinite universe and divine truths. You will find this theory developed at length in Plotinus, in St. Bonaventure, in St. Teresa, in St. Martin, and in Sweden-

[1] See "Séraphita."

borg. When Balzac dropped his microscope he became a Swedenborgian; he
said force was the great difficulty of simple logicians, "purely abstractive beings,"
as he called them; and claimed that the
finest specimens of human genius abandoned the shadows of abstraction to
reach the pure light of intuition. "The
intuitive is necessarily the most perfect
expression of man, the ring which binds
the visible world to the superior worlds.
He acts, sees, and feels through his
interior being." I do not know whether
he prays much, but he speaks of prayer
after the fashion of the *illuminated*. "The
final phase of life, that in which are sum-
med up all the others, whither tend all
the forces, and whose merits can unlock
the holy gate to the perfect being, is the
life of prayer. . . . Like the rushing
wind or the thunderbolt, it pierces
through all obstacles and participates in
the power of God. You are endowed with
the swiftness of spirit; you can transport

235

yourself in an instant throughout the regions of space; like the word you may be wafted from one end of the world to the other. It is a harmony in which you participate! It is a light, and you behold it! It is a melody which finds in you an answering chord. Under its influence you feel your intelligence developing, enlarging, and its range of sight attaining prodigious distances; in truth there is neither time nor place for the mind. . . . Although these things take place in calm and silence, without agitation, without external motion, nevertheless, in prayer all is action, but vital action stripped of all substantiality and reduced to pure being, like the motion of worlds—a force invisible and pure."

This is the theory of ecstasy; you may judge to what beauties and what dreams it will give birth. The conclusion of "Séraphita" resembles a canto of Dante; its doctrine at bottom remains Christian; human destiny is presented as a series of

236

ascending lives where the soul, guided
first "by self-love, then by the love of
being and lastly by the love of Heaven,
traverses in turn the natural world, the
spiritual world, and the divine world."
But the doctrine is clothed with all the
splendors of hallucination and poetry;
Heaven is revealed in a confused and
magnificent vision as a sort of ocean of
light in which are immersed the worlds,
robed in gold and surrounding the mys-
terious and glorious Moving-Principle
who communicates to them life and love.
"Their senses drink in the strains of
living music poured forth from the di-
verse realms of the infinite; and each
time the harmony is felt like an immense
respiration, the worlds caught in this universal movement incline toward the
mighty Being who from his central and
impenetrable depths causes all to issue
forth, and draws all to himself. . . . .
Light engenders music, music is born of
light, color is light and music, motion is

237

number endowed with the word; then, in fine, all is harmonious, diaphanous, mobile; in such manner that each substance is interpenetrated by the other; extension has no limits, and the angels traverse the abysms of the infinite. There reigns eternal joy. Myriads of angels assemble in a single flight, without confusion, all equal, all dissimilar, simple as the rose in the fields, immense as worlds. They neither appear nor vanish; they are sown in the fields of the infinite like the stars that shine in the indiscernible ether."

Such are the fantastic dreams and beliefs that his genius verges upon. To explain them he abuses romance, as Shakespeare abused the drama, imposing upon it more than it could bear. Shakespeare, oppressed by a superfluous abundance of poetry, filled his plays with cantatas, interludes, conceits, and the whole choir of innocent-shameless children of a rich and fanciful imagination.

Balzac, oppressed by a superabundance of theories, puts into his novels politics, psychology, metaphysics and the whole brood of his philosophical children, both legitimate and illegitimate.

Many persons become fatigued with it all, and condemn "Seraphita" and "Louis Lambert" as crude dreams, difficult to read. They would have a philosophy less romantic, or romances less philosophic. They complain that they are not sufficiently instructed or amused; they demand more interest and less argument. They fail to observe that these works crown the whole work as the flower crowns the plant, that the genius of the artist here finds its complete expression and its final development; that all the rest of his work is a preparation for these ideas, supposes them, explains them, and justifies them, that a cherry tree must produce cherries, a philosopher theories, and a romancer romances.

II

In Paris they make epigrams upon everything and it is the fashion to sum up ideas in frequent expression; here are some that I have collected on Balzac:

"He is the Dupuytren Museum in folio."

"He is a beautiful mushroom of the hospital."

"He is a medical Molière."

"He is the Saint-Simon of the people."

I should say more simply: With Shakespeare and Saint-Simon, Balzac is the greatest storehouse of documents on human nature that we possess.

www.ingramcontent.com/pod-product-compliance
Lightning Source LLC
Chambersburg PA
CBHW030922090426
42737CB00007B/282